Perspectives on the Impact, Mission and Purpose of the Business School

With contributions from some of the leading thinkers in business school education, this book explores the impact and purpose of the business school, and addresses some of the most important questions facing management education today.

The diverse perspectives brought together by the EFMD in this volume examine a number of common questions, themes and challenges. These include: whether business schools should be viewed as schools of management, given the complexity of the business environment; what is the positive impact of business school research, and the balance of relevant, practical impact and academic rigour; the strategic evolution of business schools and how they may evolve in a more purposeful direction; and why business school leaders compete strongly but are reluctant to collaborate, and how collaboration may encourage greater positive societal impact. With insightful commentary and illustrative case studies, this book serves as a landmark publication on the value and impact of business schools.

The book will be of particular interest to those working in business schools, higher education leaders, policy makers and business leaders seeking insight into the value, impact and future of business and management education.

Eric Cornuel is President at EFMD Global.

Howard Thomas was the inaugural Ahmass Fakahany Distinguished Professor of Global Leadership at the Questrom School, Boston University. He is also an Emeritus Professor and former Dean at Singapore Management University and a Senior Advisor at EFMD.

Matthew Wood is Director, Operations and Global Focus Magazine Editor at EFMD Global.

EFMD Management Education

This series is published in collaboration with EFMD Global.

Perspectives on the Impact, Mission and Purpose of the Business School
Edited by Eric Cornuel, Howard Thomas and Matthew Wood

For more information about this series, please visit: www.routledge.com/EFMD-Management-Education/book-series/EFMD

Perspectives on the Impact, Mission and Purpose of the Business School

Edited by
Eric Cornuel, Howard Thomas and
Matthew Wood

Routledge
Taylor & Francis Group
LONDON AND NEW YORK

Designed cover image: © Jebens Design

First published 2023
by Routledge
4 Park Square, Milton Park, Abingdon, Oxon OX14 4RN

and by Routledge
605 Third Avenue, New York, NY 10158

Routledge is an imprint of the Taylor & Francis Group, an informa business

British Library Cataloguing-in-Publication Data
A catalogue record for this book is available from the British Library

Library of Congress Cataloging-in-Publication Data
Names: Cornuel, Eric, editor. | Thomas, Howard, 1943– editor. |
    Wood, Matthew, 1970– editor.
Title: Perspectives on the impact, mission and purpose of the business school /
    Eric Cornuel, Howard Thomas, Matthew Wood, editors.
Description: Abingdon, Oxon ; New York, NY : Routledge, 2024. | Includes
    bibliographical references.
Identifiers: LCCN 2023009866 (print) | LCCN 2023009867 (ebook) |
    ISBN 9781032487588 (hardback) | ISBN 9781032487595 (paperback) |
    ISBN 9781003390633 (ebook)
Subjects: LCSH: Business education. | Business schools. | Management—
    Study and teaching.
Classification: LCC HF1106 .P46 2024 (print) | LCC HF1106 (ebook) |
    DDC 650.07/1—dc23/eng/20220124
LC record available at https://lccn.loc.gov/2023009866
LC ebook record available at https://lccn.loc.gov/2023009867

ISBN: 978-1-032-48758-8 (hbk)
ISBN: 978-1-032-48759-5 (pbk)
ISBN: 978-1-003-39063-3 (ebk)

DOI: 10.4324/9781003390633

Designed and typeset in Roboto by Jebens Design

Publisher's note
This book has been prepared from camera-ready copy provided by the author(s)/editor(s).

Contents

Global Focus:
Annual Research Volume 1 2022

Perspectives on the Impact, Mission
and Purpose of the Business School

*Eric Cornuel, Howard Thomas and
Matthew Wood - Editors*

Editors
Eric Cornuel
Howard Thomas
Matthew Wood

Design & Art Direction
Jebens Design / www.jebensdesign.co.uk

Photographs & Illustrations
©Jebens Design Ltd / EFMD unless otherwise stated

www.globalfocusmagazine.com
www.efmd.org

©EFMD
Rue Gachard 88 – Box 3,
1050 Brussels, Belgium

More ways to read *Global Focus* publications

Go to
globalfocusmagazine.com
to access the online library
of *Global Focus* publications

Your say

We are always pleased to hear your
thoughts on our publications.

Please address comments and
ideas to Matthew Wood at EFMD:
matthew.wood@efmdglobal.org

Perspectives on the Impact, Mission and Purpose of the Business School

HOWARD THOMAS

Introduction

The business school has been an important success story in the evolution of the modern university. Yet it is increasingly valued in that context "much more for its managerial expertise, cash generation ability and financial strength than its intellectual vigour and scholarship. Indeed … its legitimacy as a serious academic discipline is critically questioned by scholars in science, arts and the humanities" (Thomas, Lorange and Sheth, 2013, pp 52/3).

Rakesh Khurana (2007) argues that business schools have become the 'hired hands' of business and have abandoned any pretence of fulfilling goals of developing a cadre of professional managers as proposed by early deans (e.g. Dean Donham at Harvard Business School). Therefore, when business schools evolved into "businesses" they framed their mission and vision around a dominant paradigm, a market-based view focused on market efficiency and the principle of shareholder value maximisation – essentially 'market managerialism' (Locke and Spender, 2011). However, after a number of catastrophic business failures such as Enron, the late Sumantra Ghoshal (2005) and other critics argued that business schools in their desire to be acknowledged as legitimate and serious academic players, had been guilty of perpetuating and teaching 'amoral theories' that destroyed sound managerial practices and produced profit-maximising managers and professionals. This, in turn, may have contributed to ethical and moral behavioural lapses in events such as the global financial crisis. A key consequence was that the principle of trust central to the operation of market capitalism has been called into question.

It is clear that the global financial crisis (Harney and Thomas, 2020) and other more recent events, such as the COVID-19 pandemic and Ukraine disruptions, have been watersheds, in the strategic thinking of many participants in the management education field. A paper on re-thinking and re-evaluating the purpose of a business school (Thomas, 2017) points out that there has been a turning point and a second curve in the evolution of the field which has led to the need for change, innovation and adaptation of existing models of management education. Even more important and significant is the increasing evidence from management students in the U.S. and Europe that they value an increased business school emphasis on debates about purposeful work such as tackling ethical and moral issues of corporate social responsibility, poverty, inequality, social justice, sustainability, globalisation, climate change and inclusive growth. This focus on the so-called "people and planet" agenda has unleashed a renewed 'stakeholder' perspective in the field advocating the search for good outcomes for a broader range of stakeholders rather than simple wealth maximisation for shareholders.

Thus, there has been a growing sense that the dominant model of market capitalism may have failed indicating a future in which a more balanced mix of capitalism and purposeful inclusive models addressing multi-stakeholder growth should be closely examined (see for example the discussions of the re-evaluation of capitalism in Henderson (2020), Mayer (2018) and Mazzucato (2013, 2018)).

The British Academy (2021) has also contributed significantly to this emerging debate on the purpose of a business school by both examining the concept of a purposeful business school in business and management education and, more recently, investigating what, and how, business schools should teach, grow and develop. As a consequence, greater attention has been directed towards developing more balanced and holistic frameworks and models of management education with a higher purpose that nurture social responsibility and reinforce students understanding of ethical and moral managerial issues.

It is interesting to note that because of the cultural and contextual differences between Europe and the U.S., European management schools have already adopted a somewhat more balanced, socially responsible educational

DOI: 10.4324/9781003390633-1

Global Focus **Annual Research** Volume 1

Perspectives on the Impact, Mission and Purpose of the Business School
Howard Thomas
....

model than the more dominant U.S. paradigm of logical positivism in which theoretically-oriented research professors are valued highly. However, just as there is no universal U.S. model paradigm so there is no common European model. Indeed, there is a welcome diversity in modelling approaches reflected in the viewpoints and research papers presented in this special issue. These papers examine a number of common themes and challenges including: First, asking whether business schools should be viewed as schools of management given that the business environment is an interlocking ecosystem involving business, government, civil society and not-for-profit organisations; second, examining what is the impact of business schools in terms of the search for meaningful new ideas and positive impacts in knowledge generation and dissemination across the business ecosystem; third, addressing the processes by which schools may change and evolve in a more purposeful direction; fourth, questioning, why business school leaders generally compete strongly but are reluctant to collaborate in order to create shared value for the greater benefit of countries and regions, particularly in emerging/developing market contexts; fifth, using the virtues of the ecosystem advantage (Williamson and De Meyer, 2012) so that business school ecosystem(s) may be more carefully exploited allowing collective "know-how" to be shared to encourage greater positive, societal impact.

BUSINESS SCHOOLS, SCHOOLS FOR BUSINESS OR SCHOOLS OF MANAGEMENT

The volume starts with an updated version of a paper given initially as an after dinner speech by Professor Eric Cornuel, the President of EFMD, at the Rotterdam School of Management. After two decades at the helm of EFMD, Eric reflected on the much broader influence that EFMD and management schools, should have on global issues and the increasingly complex social, economic and political business environment. In particular, he points to the rise of nationalism and populism in the geo-political sphere which serves to entrench poverty and inequality, insecurity, and stalls inclusive growth in society across generations. He advocates stakeholder rather than shareholder value maximisation so that both schools and their faculty can advance ideas that benefit society as well as the scientific mission of academia. He champions the concept of "engaged scholarship" (Hoffman, 2021) pioneered by scholars such as Andrew Pettigrew and Andy Van de Ven and which can lead to a more responsible vision for research as well as a more inspiring educational pedagogy with the adoption of hybrid technologically-enabled

instructional methods for all forms of university and life-long learning. A quote from Hoffman captures the spirit, purpose and meaning of academic scholarship: "I want my research, teaching and outreach to have positive impact on the world around me." He also addresses the question of the meaningful impact of research when he says "citation counts, A* level publication and an h-index pale in comparison to that simple outcome (i.e. impact on the world)." Cornuel also reinforces this positive impact goal by emphasising the paramount importance of business and management schools creating meaningful, positive impact by producing research findings which can be understood and implemented by practising managers.

Kai Peters and Howard Thomas make the case for schools of management rather than business schools. They argue that the complexity of the business environment requires careful thinking about the appropriate cognitive framing of a model with the business/management schools acting as "hubs" for an ecosystem in which individuals, business, government, civil society and not-for-profits interact and co-evolve their capabilities, roles and investments to create both shareholder and stakeholder value for business and society. Hence, they propose that schools of management should embrace both disciplinary and interdisciplinary viewpoints in managing faculty, research and teaching in order to address globally important challenges such as inequality and climate change and to solve practical problems (e.g. well-being and the future of work) whose impact cuts across different stakeholders and management disciplines. They stress the theme of interdisciplinarity in educating professional managers and their vision of the growth of a professional and ethical manager as a core purpose of a management school. Their concept of a school of management is illustrated, and developed, through their historical discussion of the growth and evolution of the business school in the U.S. after WWII, which pivoted away from the original concept of educating professional managers envisaged by early business school deans to a dominant paradigm anchored around shareholder wealth management-oriented curricula. These newly emergent curricula and models favoured analytic approaches and theories, largely drawn from economics and operations research, resulting in a dominant, logical, positivist guiding paradigm which anchored the field until the early years of the current century. As already noted, events such as the global financial crisis and consequent social unrest prompted a move for transformative change in management schools involving a more balanced and wide-ranging responsible management perspective for the educational models of schools of management. These

Global Focus **Annual Research** Volume 1

Perspectives on the Impact, Mission and Purpose of the Business School
Howard Thomas
....

included addressing the impacts of technological change, economic and global change and political change movements such as nationalism and populism, which could create barriers to improvements in social justice and inclusive growth.

WHAT IS THE POSITIVE IMPACT OF BUSINESS/ MANAGEMENT SCHOOL RESEARCH?

There are a series of papers addressing the impact of research in business schools and questioning its value for practising managers. Critics have pointed out that business school academics research the wrong things often focusing on rigorous theoretical topics rather than more practical, impactful topics. For example, they argue that academics give more attention to analytical, mechanistic management tools than the softer skills of management, empathy and leadership. So, there are legitimate concerns about the balance between a rigorous pattern of academic research and the significant, **relevant** impact of the research to practice and society in terms of research on such grand challenges as inequality, social and financial exclusion, climate change and inclusive economic growth.

However, the so-called rigour/relevance debate continues unabated in the business school environment. **Academic scholars** largely measure their excellence in terms of citation counts in top (A*) journals (e.g. Google Scholar, ResearchGate, Scopus, etc.) derived from journal lists which rate journals primarily on their academic merit (e.g. impact factors). The underlying problem is that very often business school academics are evaluated primarily in terms of their publications in top journals and their employers, and deans, are judged on their ability to attract such top scholars. The critical issue is that these A* journal papers are neither being read extensively by other academics or, more importantly, by practising managers and leaders seeking insights or guidelines to improve their effectiveness.

Other scholars are, however, enhancing their "relevance" credentials by embracing such initiatives as RRBM (the Responsible Research in Business and Management community) and stressing not only academic quality but a renewed attack on purpose and responsibility to society through addressing societal grand challenges. Therefore, to the rigour/relevance criteria they would add strictures about the diffusion and meaningful, positive impact of their research to business, government and society as well as creating innovative and insightful research findings.

Anne Tsui is the legendary founder of what she describes as an instrument for transformative research changes, namely, the Responsible Research in Business and Management (RRBM) network. From its founding in 2015

(under the auspices of EFMD) with 28 founding, influential scholars dedicated to close the research-practice (rigour/ relevance) gap, the RRBM network has expanded exponentially in terms of members, co-signees, RRBM awards and journal special issues. The extent of this growth and its implications are outlined in her paper cataloguing RRBM's initial position of celebrating "small wins and calling bold actions" to quickly achieving big wins and significant, meaningful outcomes. Thus, Anne and her co-authors Mary Jo Bitner and Serguei Netessine outline the extensive current RRBM output and pose the question "What topics should business research focus on?"

Michel Kalika (the founder of the Business School Impact System (BSIS) at EFMD) and Eric Cornuel (President of EFMD) stress the critical importance of measuring not just excellent academic outputs but also all types of management impact. Based on the experience of the BSIS programme in their evaluations of around 70 EFMD member schools over the past decade, they identify six important impact channels ranging from teaching (e.g. case studies) and research (books, academic and practical papers) to impacts on local companies, regions and governments. They also assessed the dissemination of findings in academic, professional and media outlets and conferences.

What is clear from this paper is that BSIS has convincingly made a case for assessing carefully the range of positive impacts that global business schools have already generated. As a consequence, business school impact is now widely discussed in the management field. It has a long and controversial history. Professor Andrew Pettigrew's notions of a "double-hurdle" (rigour and relevance) and co-production of knowledge between academics and practical managers have been guiding principles for management researchers. Debates about the rigour/relevance criteria still continue with business and management schools increasingly searching for "meaningful impact" with their various stakeholder constituencies in order to grow their reputational capital, identity and legitimacy.

It is clear that the pursuit of research impact is a hot topic for not only business schools but also for students, researchers and governments (e.g. the periodic government-sponsored U.K. Research Excellence Funding (REF) Framework which has a significant proportion devoted to research impact). It has also recently attracted the publication, with sponsorship from the British Academy of Management (BAM), of books by Professor Usha Haley (2022) examining the U.S. impact perspective and Professor Robert McIntosh et al (2021) the U.K. perspective. In particular, Haley surveyed 20,000 global members of the U.S. academy of management and reported that the top 5

Global Focus **Annual Research** Volume 1

Perspectives on the Impact, Mission and Purpose of the Business School
Howard Thomas
....

indicators of research impact, according to both faculty and business school deans, were, in order, publishing in A* journals, counting citations for their research, gaining research grants, publishing research monographs (or books) and publishing in practitioner journals. Clearly, scholarly impact dominates practical impact in routine, research evaluation and promotion reviews in business/ management schools!

In this volume, two other papers by Gerry Johnson and Ken Starkey, and Alan Irwin provide an excellent analysis of key rigour/relevance and impact issues. The dilemma for academic researchers according to Johnson and Starkey is that they are "willingly or unwillingly" trapped in a Weberian "iron cage" about the publication imperative, namely, the pressure to publish in the A* journals. This pressure is reinforced by the seeming reluctance of well-regarded and prestigious scholars, or indeed deans, to abandon research performance criteria based primarily on citation metrics and in which quality judgement criteria based on rigour in research methodology and novel theory dominate the relevance of the chosen research area. It should be noted that these authors do not argue for the primacy of relevance and impact over first-rate academic scholarship. They point out that both are needed in business and management research.

Alan Irwin reinforces the importance of the rigour and relevance criteria but prefers to augment the "great divide", namely, the apparent separation between academic excellence and practical application in the conduct of the business of research in business schools. He argues, very much in the spirit of the papers of Eric Cornuel and Kai Peters / Howard Thomas that it is the right time for business schools "to take stock of what they are for". He wants to open up thinking about the future of business schools in terms of the themes of seriously addressing the key issues of purpose, responsibility and quality. Thus, one of the important elements in contemplating future business school scenarios is the need to examine in granular detail the relationships, and necessary dialogues that should be undertaken, between business school researchers, those from other disciplines and the problems of larger society. He notes that already societal impact research has seen serious engagement around issues of sustainability, society inequality and business transformation. He also points out the importance of work undertaken by Martin Kitchener and colleagues from the Chartered Association of Business Schools in the U.K. in outlining current findings about public value in their publication "Business Schools and the Public Good" (Kitchener et al, 2021).

STRATEGIC CHANGE IN BUSINESS SCHOOLS: PURPOSE, INTERDISCIPLINARITY

Indeed, Martin Kitchener, with Rachel Ashworth (the current Dean of Cardiff) demonstrate very clearly the importance of public good concerns in their paper explaining how they have re-engineered Cardiff Business School. Cardiff is well-regarded as a business /management school focusing on the public good – one of the first examples of U.K. schools (which also include Birmingham, Glasgow Caledonian, Manchester, the University of the Arts London, Queen Mary University, London and Queen's Belfast). They address very clearly how business schools can better contribute to society by adopting the corporate purpose of "generating profitable solutions for the problems of people and planet, while not profiting from creating problems for either".

Kitchener outlines clearly how CARBS (Cardiff Business School) framed the vision of 'a public value business school' around John Brewer's thesis on the public value of social science. Their subsequent strategy formulation process, a template for a purpose-driven school, involved consultation with an extensive range of internal CARBS colleagues and external partners – advisory boards, university and government leaders and employers. The result of this process was the CARBS mission statement to

"Promote economic and social improvement through interdisciplinary scholarship that addresses the grand challenges of our time, while operating a strong and progressive approach to our own governance."

Alongside the mission statement, the school's purpose-oriented strategic choices involving purposeful teaching (with a moral/ethical compass), purposeful interdisciplinary research, purposeful engagement (with an international board and monthly local breakfast topic-oriented meetings) and purposeful governance (with an innovative "shadow cabinet") are outlined.

The theme of interdisciplinary and change is also evident in the engaging use by Qua and Sporn of social network analysis in the introduction and development of interdisciplinary programmes in two different country and cultural contexts. The use of social network analysis, and network science, is novel and focuses not only on contextual influences but also social capital networks of relating bonding and linking (Nahapiet and Ghoshal, 1998) as social influences on the implementation of these programmes.

Lee, Thomas and Wilson's paper builds upon ideas of purposeful identity and interdisciplinarity in programme design. It examines the evolution of a new management university – Singapore Management University (SMU) – from a strategic perspective. It tracks the genesis of the idea of a third local Singaporean University in the late 1990s, to the founding strategy of SMU in 2000, and finally to its profile and ambitions in 2020 and beyond – in essence, a study of its emergence as a school of liberal social science-oriented management studies focussing particularly on what it has achieved and where it is going?

The study of strategic evolution involved data gathering about SMU and its actions, identifying patterns of strategic evolution over defined periods of time (change milestones, e.g. start-up, growth, etc.) and analysing both secondary data and interviews with key individuals (e.g. deans, provost/presidents) to draw conclusions and deconstruct the value chains, leadership and business model processes of SMU. Note that there are very few similar studies of either business schools or their professional organisations (e.g. AACSB, EFMD, etc.) that have undertaken such granular, detailed strategic processual analysis. Typically most comparable studies have been written as celebrations of anniversaries (e.g. Barsoux (2000) for INSEAD or the 25th EFMD anniversary volume ("Training the Fire Brigade", 1996)) and contain well-written reflections on elements of progress but are not critical analyses of strategic evolution and development attempting to draw conclusions about organisational leadership, strategies and patterns of strategic change as the organisation evolves through time.

In summary, the SMU study demonstrates that SMU is regarded as an important educational "hub" in Singapore's business and educational ecosystem. It is seen as an interdisciplinary catalyst which facilitates student and faculty interaction with government, public agencies, business and professional organisations and through action-based, experiential learning produces responsible students, and managers, who, in turn, can address, attack and achieve Singapore's targets for inclusive social and economic growth.

COLLABORATION, COMPETITION AND WELL-BEING

How can business schools work together on collaborative issues such as mental health and well-being and interactive curriculum developments about equality and diversity rather than being forced into a "competitive fetish" by media rankings and 'publish and perish' citation counts?

Sir Cary Cooper (Manchester) is without doubt one of the legendary figures in the development of business and management education in the U.K.. As an organisational psychologist he has been at the forefront of debates about gross national wellbeing and the future of work. He stresses that the real challenge for senior managers is to create well-being cultures. He is at the forefront of a continuing effort to build awareness through regular meetings of a council/committee drawn from both well-known business school academics and senior business leaders who meet

regularly to address timely issues associated with the future of work and flexible working that have been particularly evident during the Covid pandemic. His additional chairmanship of a group of BAM fellows is leading to the development of well-being policies for U.K. business schools and their constituents.

Collaboration across schools in the LATAM area is the topic of Gabriela Alvarado's paper. She has championed strong collaboration among schools in the Latin America Region with the aim of sharing collective know-how about teaching and research so that a distinctive framework for Latin American schools can be formulated and enhanced. In particular, with the support of EFMD, she has set up a virtual LATAM research network with the aim of building collaborative research networks and programmes that will benefit the intellectual growth and identity of LATAM schools. This network complements other collaborative efforts championed by the CLADEA and BALAS organisations conferences which together develop meaningful long-term collaborations among LATAM schools.

Rajani Naidoo and Jürgen Enders discuss how competitive and collaborative forces can act together to improve the quality of business schools globally despite the current strength of competitive forces in the management education world.

Their paper on the competitive "fetish" is both provocative and insightful. It argues that there is a competition orthodoxy in business schools which may impede the development of socially responsible models of management education. This competition fetish means that "business schools appear to be trapped in a modern-day magical belief that competition will provide the solution to all problems. Competition is expected to enhance quality in research and lead to real world impact." In essence, competition may wrongly be perceived as the magic bullet.

The authors point out that a range of different competitive forces have increasingly been imposed on business schools. For example, governmental level research excellence contests (such as the recent Research Excellence Framework (REF) in the U.K.), combine with media rankings (such as the Financial Times (with its ranking criteria including the so-called FT-50 Top Journal lists)) and a citation and publishing industry (e.g. Google Scholar, ResearchGate, Scopus) to construct worldwide measures of the quality of business school research. Such measures can lead to increasing isomorphism among business schools reinforced with a range of associated reputational rankings in the form of league tables which tend to define competitive behaviour and resulting strategic actions.

Global Focus **Annual Research** Volume 1

Perspectives on the Impact, Mission and Purpose of the Business School
Howard Thomas
....

However, they also emphasise that these very narrow competitive league tables are often grounded in faculty citation measures in top journals (largely North American but occasionally European journals). These, in turn, tend to devalue the impact, and importance, of other contributions to the management education field. They stress the need for research diversity in valuing meaningful research efforts including influential books, research monographs and applied, practitioner-oriented papers, as well as projects that seek to research such issues as inequality, poverty and inclusive growth. They believe that "competition unthinkingly deployed everywhere can lead to negative consequences which act as barriers to business schools contributing to the greater good." A good example is their concern, also identified by a leading African scholar, Stella Nkomo, that research about the issues/challenges and crises "facing the majority of the world's population living in low-income countries receive less attention." Indeed, this is a clear plea to recognise that management education is a global industry in which collaboration and mutual recognition of different challenges is an absolute imperative. Therefore, a strong understanding of content, country, context and culture must also be nurtured and recognised in developing alternative management education models, and research impacts, across the globe.

Looking to the future they hope that business schools will adopt research strategies such as Bath's "Research 4 Good" initiatives as well as initiatives for responsible research promoted by Anne Tsui's Responsible Research Community. In addition, they believe that an increasing research focus on responsible management education and sustainability will lead to the development of, and experimentation with, more holistic and critical models of management education across national contexts with the purpose of developing "global citizens with critical reasoning while enhancing students' abilities to respond to some of the most serious threats that democracy faces."

IMD'S PERSPECTIVES ON BUSINESS SCHOOL, MISSION, IMPACT AND PURPOSE

The concept of how the impact, mission, purpose, and value of a management school should be formulated is often delegated to the dean, faculty and advisory committees in most schools. We deliberately selected a school, IMD, which is both highly regarded and has an excellent reputation to identify how strategic issues of the impact, purpose and value of a business school are translated in practice. IMD's stance and mission is perhaps closer to the ideal of a highly practically-oriented school which exemplifies rigour, relevance and impact in terms of strongly applied research findings than a more research-oriented management school. Its director, Jean-Francois Manzoni draws out clearly how its strategic positioning provides insights and implementation guidelines both in Switzerland and more generally to its global constituents and ecosystem participants.

IMD's values as a hub in its ecosystem serving business, governmental and societal stakeholders are that it is an engaged, scholarly partner in creating positive, meaningful and impactful outcomes for its stakeholders internally (with regard to its strong faculty) and externally (with its strong knowledge generation and dissemination). In essence, IMD is a 'networking' organisation whose impacts include excellent teaching and pedagogy, applied pragmatic research of rigour, relevance, insights and global reach as well as policy and consulting outputs about world competitiveness and global challenges such as inequality and sustainability. Nevertheless, it is constantly renewing and refreshing its structure to achieve "strong, shared understanding of the school's purpose, economic model, culture and values." In other words, to use Drucker's well-known quote "culture eats strategy for breakfast."

References

Barsoux, P. (2000) *From Intuition to Institution*. London: Palgrave Macmillan

The British Academy (2021) *Business and Management Provision in U.K. Higher Education*. London: British Academy Publications

EFMD (1996) *Training in the Fire Brigade: Preparing for the Unimaginable*. Brussels: EFMD Publications

Ghoshal, S. (2005) Bad management theories are destroying good management practices. *Academy of Management Learning and Education*, 4(1), pp.75-91

Haley, U. (2022) *Impact and the Management Researcher*. Abingdon: Routledge

Harney, S. and H. Thomas (2020) *The Liberal Arts and Management Education: A Global Agenda for Change*. Cambridge: Cambridge University Press

Henderson, R. (2020) *Re-imagining Capitalism in a world on fire*. Cambridge, MA: Harvard Business School Press

Hoffman, A. (2021) *The Engaged Scholar: Expanding the impact of Academic Research in Today's World*. Stanford, CA: Stanford University Press

Khurana, R. (2007) *From Higher Aims to Hired Hands: The Social Transformation of American Business Schools and the Unfulfilled Promise of Management as a Profession*. Princeton, NJ: Princeton University Press

Global Focus **Annual Research** Volume 1

Perspectives on the Impact, Mission and Purpose of the Business School
Howard Thomas
....

Locke, R.R., and Spender, J. C. (2011) *Confronting Managerialism: How the business elite and their schools threw our lives out of balance*. London: Zed Books Ltd

Kitchener, M. (2021) *Business Schools and the Public Good*. London: CABS Publications

Mayer, C. (2018) *Prosperity: Better business makes the greater good*. Oxford: Oxford University Press

Mazzucato, M. (2013) *The Entrepreneurial State: Debunking Private and Public Sector Myths*. London: Anthem Press

Mazzucato, M (2018) *The Value of Everything: Making and taking in the global economy*. London: Allen Lane, Penguin Books

McIntosh, R., Mason, K., Beech, N., and Bartunek, J.M. (2021) *Delivering Impact in Management Research: When does it really happen*. Abingdon: Routledge

Nahapiet, J. and Ghoshal, S. (1998) Social capital, intellectual capital, and the organisational advantage. *Academy of Management Review, 23*(2), pp. 242-266

Thomas, H., P. Lorange and J Sheth (2013) *The Business School in the 21st Century: Emergent Challenges and New Business Models*. Cambridge: Cambridge University Press

Williamson, P.J. and De Meyer, A (2012) Ecosystem Advantage: How to harness the power of partners. *California Management Review, 55*(1), Fall 2012, pp. 24-46

About the Author

Howard Thomas is the Dean of Fellows at the British Academy of Management, Emeritus Professor at Singapore Management University and Senior Advisor at EFMD Global.

Positive Impact: An Important Role for Business School Leadership in a Changing, Precarious World

ERIC CORNUEL

The COVID-19 crisis and the Ukraine war makes it more important than ever to take a more global approach to recovery

The pandemic left little choice but to throw learning institutions into a period of transformation and change. Disruption in the learning modalities unfolded, bringing digital platforms to the fore and sparking new innovative methods to further academic goals.

It was not only a moment of an accelerated tactical adaptation for us, but also a moment of profound strategic reflection about our mission, purpose and values. This requirement for strategic reflection has been further emphasised by the global turmoil resulting from the Ukraine war.

One of the key issues is the return to the sources of impact that business education can have on its environment. For example, the disruption brought by the pandemic prepares ground for a new mandate for higher education institutions which looks at how institutions can have an even more **significant positive impact** on societies and ecosystems, but also how they can integrate into them even more harmoniously and effectively. Management schools and educators should not be passive observers; they must contribute more by addressing global challenges in an increasingly complex environment. And there are many more global issues that need to be tackled with quite some urgency.

You can feel the increasing tensions that exist today among a diverse range of people. Dangerous political phenomena are part of the equation. We notice an important disconnection between the political world and the rest of society that is very detrimental to trust in institutions and democratic systems. The Edelman Trust Barometer shows that trust in elites has eroded immensely, and people across all social strata have lost trust in politicians, big business, financial institutions and the media. The 2021 results revealed an epidemic of misinformation and widespread mistrust of societal institutions and leaders around the world.

And these sentiments are not surprising. The burden of the 2008 financial crisis has been largely taken on by citizens, which has left some with the impression that the financial sector is above the law. When the system started to crack and everything eventually collapsed, people felt that society picked up the pieces. Karl Marx said that the end of capitalism will come from finance. I'm not a Marxist by any means, but in light of current events, it seems he was not far off the truth.

A lack of leadership in political and business governance results in the rise of anxiety and stress, unemployment and societal defragmentation. We risk seeing ever more disenchanted and angry citizens of all generations forming a precariat, or precarious proletariat, so well described by Guy Standing. These are people who do not enjoy stable employment, rising income and a sense of belonging.

The growing precariat is coupled with a shrinking middle class. The famous 'elephant chart' designed by the economist and demographer, Branko Milanović, shows that in Western countries, people at the very top of the income distribution realise huge gains while the poorest, sitting quite figuratively at the bottom of the tail, have seen marginal improvements. The paradox here is that while global poverty has marginally improved, the gap (or disparity) between the rich and the poor has widened significantly across the world according to the World Bank's most recent data. Unfortunately, in between sits the "shrinking" middle class.

Another complementary phenomenon is the stalling of economic mobility across generations. The next generations are not moving up the income ladder, which was a perceivable trend since the end of WWII. We must correct this erosion of generational mobility by taking meaningful and strong action against the dominance, at least in practice, of the shareholder value model.

In fact, the shareholder value model, which emerged strongly after the Second World War in the U.S., is more recent than the stakeholder model. However people embraced a much broader societal role for the corporation at that time and this ethos is re-emerging in the mainstream discourse now, and for good reasons. As business schools, we must actively advocate for a compassionate, stakeholder value model. One of the critical issues for companies as well as for organisations such as ours, is to raise awareness and embrace a cohesive, socio-economic ecosystem approach; but this requires a paradigm shift towards the view that business schools should have a purposeful mission to create value and **positive, meaningful societal impacts** for their ecosystem partners.

Business schools, therefore, have a critical role to play to rewire our missions for relevance and impact, and to be close to the needs and address real issues of society and economy. At EFMD, we have been strong advocates of a broader, inclusive approach to the impactful role of business and management education, and we try to encourage business schools and companies to follow this route of stakeholder focussed responsible management education. Indeed, our strong founding sponsorship and continuing advocacy of the goals of the RRBM network is fundamental to our continued search for positive impact. Further over the last decade, EFMD has itself co-created significant practical ecosystem impacts. The EFMD "Excellence in Practice" awards have generated case studies of positive practical insights and, EFMD's "BSIS" impact audits of over 70 leading business schools have demonstrated clearly the wide range of societal impacts from those schools.

However, the underlying problem is that our current business education model favours academic research loosely coupled with societal needs. Several years ago, Christian Terwiesch and Karl Ulrich from the Wharton School estimated the cost of creating an A-Journal article at approximately 400,000 USD (about 350,000 EUR). Despite these immense amounts pouring into the systems, there is too much disconnection between research and business practice. There is an emphasis on quantity over quality and novelty over replicability. We are spending a lot of time writing papers with unclear value to practice and frankly, to knowledge. Sadly, the main motivation is often to be published in a specialist A-journal that a narrow circle of your peers reads, not to contribute to a better management of organisations or societies.

We have, of course, a scientific mission but a societal one too. The academic impact and rigorous research are important, but we also have a vital societal responsibility to produce **positive impact**. Being uniquely positioned at the intersection of social science, technology and business, and having a reasonable degree of institutional autonomy, we can contribute immensely to solving global and complex challenges such as climate change, rising inequalities, international isolationism, eroding democratic systems, and the spread of fake news.

The dominant research model must evolve fast, otherwise we may go from "publish or perish" to "publish and perish". We need to move towards an open system instead of an atomised intellectual endeavour that is constrained to narrow academic circles. We need faculty members to be engaged in, and most importantly, rewarded for applied projects, multidisciplinary, impactful research, innovation in teaching, engagement in society and communities. We need more engaged professors, as Andrew Pettigrew calls them. This is precisely a vision that we support via the Responsible Research in Business and Management (RRBM) network, initiated by Anne Tsui and supported strongly by a group of renowned scholars. I realise that the entire ecosystem including business schools, research funding agencies, publishers, ranking media outlets, and accreditation bodies have an important role to play here with an enhanced focus on positive impact as well as academic excellence.

The digital revolution and rapid hybridisation of learning experience has accelerated interesting phenomena that may pave the way for the future. We can envisage a repository of shared learning resources across business schools around the world and, in a sense, re-nobilitate the role of faculty, who instead of conveying fundamental knowledge, could devote this time to in-depth discussions and development of analytical skills among students. In other words, we don't need 100 introductory courses to accounting, but we need graduates who can think critically about the potential impact of their marketing campaigns on the trust in democratic institutions.

Lifelong learning means not only reskilling and upskilling, but also an opportunity for nurturing a closer connection between alumni and their alma mater. The faculty could enjoy a coaching and mentoring role, advising on career choices and leading intellectual exchange that goes way beyond the moment of graduation. The word faculty adopted for academia in late fourteenth century from an old French faculté, meant "ability in knowledge."

And here, there is a great role for business schools to set this strategic compass in motion. We can be a central node in an ecosystem linking higher education institutions, business and society. But I also realise how challenging and brave it is for many business schools to be at the forefront of dynamic and volatile change, operating in a complex system of stakeholders, with sometimes conflicting interests and dynamics. Our search for **significant positive impact** for our socio-economic system partners means that we will continue to evolve and strengthen the EFMD BSIS impact system, the EFMD "Practice in Excellence" awards and the analysis of positive impact through peer review in our EQUIS accreditation process. As a further example, in searching for further positive impacts, we are again co-sponsoring the "Going Beyond" awards with GBSN (the Global Business School Network) which will produce another set of excellent positive, practical and impactful research insights for our practitioner audiences.

The recent crises make it more important than ever to take a global approach to recovery. We need more international cooperation, strong positive impact, and a greater emphasis on societal issues. The question remains: is this a credible scenario? Is there room for optimism? Or will the political and economic agendas of the few push us towards a wilder capitalism driven by opportunistic and populist leaders?

I hope the former, but it's up to us, really.

About the Author

Eric Cornuel is the President of EFMD Global.

Business Schools should be Schools of Management: An Evolutionary Perspective

KAI PETERS AND HOWARD THOMAS

In the world of business schools, we do get ourselves in a muddle. Since shortly after the start of business schools in the United States around the beginning of the twentieth century following the establishment of schools of commerce decades earlier, and certainly in the last few years, business school academics and commentators have engaged in a wide-ranging debate about the mission, value and purpose of business schools.

This continuous self-criticism has taken in a range of perspectives over the years. As Pettigrew and Starkey (2016 p. 653) observe, there is a certain irony here given the prima facie success of the business school sector over the past one hundred plus years with their estimates suggesting that there are between 12,000 and 13,000 business schools of significance world-wide. Pointing to Pfeffer and Fong (2002), Mintzberg (2004) and Bennis and O'Toole (2005), they note "it seems perverse that a worldwide education industry should also attract a minor industry of challenge and skepticism from its own professoriate". This criticism and attack has focused on the business school's value and impact on society. As the late Sumantra Ghoshal (2005) notes, describing business schools as teaching amoral values that were largely absent of a moral or ethical compass and thus destroyed sound managerial practice.

In one thread of the criticism, in 2018, Martin Parker pronounced "shut down the business school". As authors, in this chapter, we would like to suggest something which is related: namely to abolish or transform business schools and replace them with schools of management. We call for this repositioning for a number of reasons:

1. Management is needed in profit, not-for-profit and public sector organisations and is particularly important in facilitating collaboration across these sectors
2. Management, whether in business, government or in the third sector needs well-trained, professional managers with capabilities in a broad range of areas such as finance, operations and strategy as well as in the handling of people and resources in a trustworthy and ethical manner
3. Management implies longer term thinking and not short-term profit maximization – it requires a concern and responsibility for the impact of decisions across significant stakeholders

This paper is structured around a number of key episodes in the development of management education. We will look at the original driving forces which led to the creation of institutions, particularly in the U.S., including the vision of their founders which would support our perspective in favour of schools of management. We will then turn to the influence of the two world wars on management and how this affected management education and how the original purpose shifted. Subsequently, we will look at the years following the Second World War and how the Ford and Carnegie 'Foundation Reports' as well as the Cold War led to further evolution away from a school of management to a business school mission. We will then look at the period roughly from 1970 to 2000 during which U.S. business school funding, which had been largely provided by the foundations, was replaced by significant donations from individuals seeking to attach their name to a prestigious business school and how this drove a further evolution away from the broad goal of a school of management to a narrow goal of the business school. Finally, we will come full circle to a reflection on how management education curricula have developed since the beginning and through the phases mentioned above. We will conclude with some thoughts on what management is actually all about and why practicing managers need "schools of management" rather than "business schools".

DOI: 10.4324/9781003390633-3

Global Focus **Annual Research** Volume 1

Business Schools should be Schools of Management: An Evolutionary Perspective
Kai Peters and Howard Thomas
....

HISTORICAL ORIGINS

Despite the existence of "Colleges of Commerce" in Europe during the 18th and 19th Centuries, the categorization and concept of management education evolved from the growing interest in management as an academic subject in the United States at the end of the 19th and beginning of the 20th Century when industrialization was in full swing. The development of railroads and transport, of basic industries like steel, mining, and oil and gas, of food production and of manufacture were all increasing in scale and complexity and at a tremendous pace. The capacity to manage in these organisations, however, lagged behind. Management was not considered a noble occupation like professions such as medicine and law. Thus, the often less intelligent and often less educated members of well-off families tended to assume management roles as a fallback: "Business has become in part a catch-all and a dumping ground into which in the case of many families' inferior sons are advised to go" (Donham 1927).

Nevertheless, over time, management became more popular among graduates of notable universities like Harvard University, the University of Pennsylvania and Dartmouth College. Once these graduates had established themselves in industry, they began petitioning their alma maters to establish graduate schools of management education and business administration. The Wharton School at Penn was established in 1881, Dartmouth's Tuck School of Business in 1900 and Harvard's Graduate School of Business Education (now Harvard Business School) was formed in 1908. These schools would "provide a setting for the education of a new kind of manager who, instilled with the sense of social obligation derived from an elite background, would run corporations in a way consistent

with the broader interests of the country" (Khurana 2007, p. 46). This progressive-style reform was to replace the robber baron practices of the founders of some of the early corporations, seeking to ensure that management was a noble and worthwhile profession which also served society more broadly. In 1916, 17 leading business schools formed the Association to Advance Collegiate Schools of Business (AACSB) in order to establish standards and to certify management as a legitimate profession.

This concern for a broader conceptualization of managerial education was broadly carried by the early deans of business schools. Writing in 1913, Leon Marshall, the fourth dean of what had been founded as the University of Chicago's College of Commerce and Politics in 1898, and renamed as the School of Commerce and Administration during his tenure, stated:

However important it may be to turn out businessmen who can make money, social workers who can command good salaries, civic workers who can rise to positions of influence and affluence, the most important task of all is to aid in promoting the progress and welfare of society. (Marshall 1913)

As late as 1933, Wallace Donham, an early Harvard Dean, sought to "train men to study general social relationships with the broad vision and the philosophic view needed" (Donham, 1933, p 435). Donham, according to Yogev, (2001), was particularly concerned by the aggressive and volatile nature of industrial relations at the time and regularly called for a progressive approach. His colleague Lawrence Lowell, viewing social relations from the societal side, reinforced the need for a stable society. He said the school would train qualified public administrators whom the government would have no choice but to employ, thereby building a better public administration. (Yogev 2001).

While the goals of early management education had been outlined in a general way in seeking to improve management and to ensure progressive labor relations and a humanistic approach, translating this to the curricular level required improvisation and led to an evolution. Some of the early subjects included classes like business English, commercial correspondence, accounts, office technique and stenography. Even by 1928, there was little agreement on what ought to be taught. Of the 34 schools studied, the only subjects they largely agreed on were Accounting, Economic Theory, English and Law. Of note are two areas which would develop in different ways over time. Among other subjects, Foreign Languages, Government, Psychology and Social Science would recede while subjects like Mathematics, Statistics and Physical Environment (Operations) would grow significantly. (Khurana 2007, p. 159).

For the latter, the experiences of the Two World Wars proved critical. In particular, U.S. business schools looked closely at the experience of their armed forces in these and other conflicts. It became obvious that strategic and logistical planning were key components for large scale activities. We will return to this development shortly. For the prior case, effectively the humanities in management, this marked a high point. As Khurana notes, there were basically three approaches to management education all competing for primacy. The first was the humanistic approach in the liberal arts tradition involving subjects like history, philosophy, English and mathematics which already existed in many universities. The second involved courses aimed at specific occupations like railroad transport, lumber management or banking. The third, which arose from the more quantitative subjects like Statistics and Operations, would subsequently be developed into an analytical and logical positivist 'science of administration'.

THE POSTWAR PERIOD

The key question which must be addressed is this section is why the third curricular path, the path of quantification, the path of the business school gained the ascendancy in the post-war period and displaced the humanistic, social science approach of the school of management that was more common in Europe and that had been advocated by Donham and colleagues at Harvard earlier.

A number of political and ideological paths need to be followed a few steps back. The first concerns the philosophical view taken by the different factions in the business school world. While Donham at Harvard was professing a *laissez-faire* humanism, Robert Maynard Hutchins, who became the President of the University of Chicago in 1929 at the age of 30, was, against his own intellectual preferences, laying the groundwork for *laissez-faire* economics. Hutchins invited the radical free market economist Friedrich Hayek to Chicago in the 1930s. The motivation was to create an intellectually exciting environment. The unintended outcome was that the University of Chicago's Business School became increasingly free-market radical and libertarian. This trend continued after the Second World War with an additional wave of free-market economists that included Richard Posner, Ronald Coase and Gary Becker, all of whom viewed not only economics, but pretty much everything else (the family, politics, crime, etc.) from an economist's rationalist point of view.

In parallel, the postwar period saw the establishment of a think-tank called the RAND Corporation. Basing itself on lessons learned in World War Two planning, RAND championed an approach whereby:

"problems of national security and extending ultimately to a wide range of public concerns" we studied with *"a focus on the use of decision-theory, mathematics, statistics, and microeconomic analysis to improve choices made by leaders of social collectives (such as armies, firms, nations)."* (Augier and March, 2011 p. 74)

Invariably, there was a lot of movement between quantitatively oriented academics in universities and RAND. This should not come as a surprise as there had been a lot of movement between academia and the US military establishment during the war. Effectively, a revolving door was established between the military, academia and RAND which continued until well into the 1960s.

Early funding for RAND came from the Ford Foundation which had been set up in 1936 from a legacy donation from the founder of the Ford Motor Company. The Ford Foundation was strongly in favour of free-market capitalism and a small state, but also in economic improvement, freedom and democracy and world peace. Similar but smaller foundations, notably the Sloan Foundation arising out of General Motors and the Carnegie Foundation arising from the steel industry, were also significant. It should be noted that by the mid-1950s, the "Foundations" were the most important source of funding for a key group of influential graduate business schools: Stanford, Harvard, Chicago, Carnegie Tech, Columbia, UCLA, UC Berkeley and MIT.

With the Foundations providing significant funding, their opinions on management education were voiced and listened to. There were a number of areas of dissatisfaction: management education seemed incoherent, it was too based on "war stories" rather than on academic rigor and too many faculty members were academically unqualified. In 1959, the Carnegie Foundation's report (the Pierson Report) and the Ford Foundation's Gordon and Howell report effectively called for the reform of business school curricula from a "wasteland of vocationalism" and unsubstantiated descriptive content to quantitative description based on rigorous data collection, computer-assisted mathematical modelling, and the foundational concepts of science: testable hypotheses, correlated observations and causal explanation (Mulligan 1987). Unsurprisingly, given the financial dependence of certainly the main funding recipients, business schools fell into line and pursued the agenda which had been set for them by the Foundations.

Another factor was instrumental in the behavior of the Foundations at the time. While Ford, Carnegie and Sloan all professed to support initiatives which encouraged education, freedom, democracy and world peace, their initiatives took place during the extreme Cold War era of Senator Joseph McCarthy and the related House Un-American Activities Committee. Both McCarthy and HUAC were convinced that there were Communist enemies within the United States, having infiltrated government, film and media, education and pretty much everywhere else. Through a number of dubious attacks on individuals and organisations, McCarthy and HUAC aggression was met by paranoia and fear by those accused.

Already in 1952, a House of Representatives Select Committee (the Reece Committee) threatened the Foundations with the removal of their tax-exempt status should they engage in activities that were un-American and subversive, or for purposes not in the interest or tradition of the United States. Hearings were held with Committee members questioning the Ford Foundation's involvement with academics and foreigners, particularly programmes in social science which implied, obviously, that this meant 'socialist' science. (Augier and March 2011, p.110). In fact, some members of the Committee accused the Foundation of showing "symptoms of inadequate anti-communism" (Augier and March 2011, p. 298).

It is thus no real wonder that the Foundations moved away from a social sciences school of management view to a more narrow business school perspective. Within business education, they clearly saw benefit in promoting the quantitative vision of management which was aligned with RAND, military and red-blooded American capitalist viewpoints, and in downplaying any interest in any humanistic, liberal, social science aspects of organisational and managerial life. Clearly academics like Economics professor George Stigler at the University of Chicago, who stated that "it is hard for me to make sense out of any concept of social responsibility which does not rely exclusively on profit maximization and conformity with the law" and who inspired the catechism that "there is only one social science, and it is economics" reflected the acceptable mood of the McCarthy era. (Augier and March 2011, p. 170).

Even some years later, another Chicago academic, Milton Friedman, wrote:

Businessmen believe that they are defending free enterprise when they declaim that business is not concerned 'merely' with profit but also with promoting desirable 'social' ends; that business has a 'social conscience' and takes seriously its responsibilities for providing employment, eliminating discrimination, avoiding pollution and whatever else may be the catchwords of the contemporary crop of reformers. In fact, they are – or would be if anyone else took the seriously – preaching pure and unadulterated socialism. (Friedman 1970).

By 1960, these trends had led to a curriculum which was distantly related to the curricula in business schools in the between-the-wars period. Capon (1996) in his prolific description of curriculum development at Columbia Business School, outlines the core curriculum in place in 1960 following these developments. Nine modules made up the core: World Resources: Physical, Technological and Human; Conceptual Foundations of Business; Business in a Dynamic Economy; Administration of the Firm; Business Decision Making; Human Behavior in Organisations, Policy Determination and Operations, and three Quantitative Methods mini modules: accounting, statistics and operations analysis. To note is that students at Columbia did not consider their school to be particularly quantitative at the time.

Nearly thirty years later in 1989, the Columbia curriculum had a core of Conceptual Foundations, Financial Accounting, Microeconomics, Macroeconomics, Organisational Behavior, Probability and Statistics, Operations Research and Management Science and Policy. Amazingly, Human Resources, Finance, Marketing and Operations were all electives. Of the 13 other major schools reviewed by Capon, the basic core was very similar to what was on offer at Columbia, but most others also required Finance, Marketing and Operations. Human Resources, Communications and

Global Focus **Annual Research** Volume 1

Business Schools should be Schools of Management: An Evolutionary Perspective
Kai Peters and Howard Thomas
....

International Business were all electives if offered at all. In the wake of McCarthyism, the Foundation Reports and the ascendancy of Economics, the social sciences had pretty much disappeared completely from the management education curriculum.

ON THE TYRANNY OF RANKINGS AND THE NAMING OF NAMES

The trend towards the quantification of management education, towards the mission of business schools promoting profit maximization, and towards a strongly pro-capitalist libertarian attitude was further reinforced by an additional development. Writing in 2005, Andy Policano, Dean Emeritus of both the business schools at the University of Wisconsin in Madison and of the business school at the University of California, Irvine stated that:

"Few people can remember what it was like before 1988 – what I call the year before the storm (of Business Week rankings). It was a time when business school deans could actually focus on improving the quality of their schools' educational offerings. Discussions about strategic marketing were confined mostly to the marketing curriculum. PR firms were hired by businesses, not business schools. Many business schools had sufficient facilities, but few buildings had marble floors, soaring atriums, or plush carpeting. Public university tuition was affordable for most students, and even top MBA programmes were accessible to students with high potential but low GMAT scores"

After 1988, unsurprisingly, ultra-competitive capitalism was not only discussed in business schools but became a feature of the environment in which business schools themselves competed. Competing on 'marble floors, soaring atriums and plush carpeting' is an expensive undertaking, and is the ever-increasing role of research and highly paid faculty members. This competitive landscape led to a search for increased sources of funding for business schools to pay for these investments.

As Burch and Nanda (2005) note, almost 50 prominent business schools were 'named' in the late 1980's and 1990's for sizable donations which supplemented tuition income and dwarfed any residual income that had been provided by the Foundations. As an aside, the authors note that as the supply of name-able schools decreases, the price on remaining name-able schools increases. This is certainly true as some of the residual schools only named since 2000 have received substantial amounts.

Of the 57 schools reviewed, the authors helpfully provide some details on the donors of each of the schools. It is, of course, a who's who of American capitalism of the 1980's and 1990's: real estate developers, investment bankers, fund managers; retail, industry, and media barons. Between 1980

and 2000, business schools at public universities received naming donations broadly in the range of $20M to $30M, while business schools at private universities generally received more. As the authors rightfully predicted, the price of naming rights has increased since 2000. Of particular note are the Booth School at Chicago which generated $300M in 2008 and the Ross School at Michigan which generated $100M in 2004. At the time of writing (January 2022), Harvard, Stanford, Yale, Columbia and a handful of other well-known US institutions remain 'nameless', it remains to be seen whether they will accept a donation and if so, for how much. Additionally, there are of course business schools elsewhere in the world that may well welcome being named.

There are a number of elements worth noting here. The first is largely philosophical and speculative. As authors, we would propose that the political orientation of many of the donors would be one of intense adherence to a pro-capitalist libertarian orientation which again promoted a narrow business school rather than broader school of management perspective. It is not our role here to attempt to gain sight of their tax returns, but one expects that they keep a close eye on their levels of taxation. The fact that they are in a position to donate substantially of course also offers them tax offsets due to their charitable donations. In the US, these can go up to significant amounts, so well-timed donations can be of significant benefit in various tax years.

The second is obviously the 'immortality' bestowed through the naming convention. From a school's perspective, it obviously helps if the donor quietly passes away and no scandals are unearthed in or after life. Unfortunate examples abound in life: the Georgia Institute of Technology was named 'DuPree' in 1996 for $25M, but the name was stripped in 2004 because the money did not arrive. It was named Scheller in 2009 for $50M. In the UK, Imperial College's business school was briefly named 'Tanaka' for £27M in 2000, but the name was removed in 2008 when a fraud scandal erupted around said Tanaka.

Death is also no salvation. The business school at City University in London was named Cass in 2002 with a donation from the Cass Foundation. Alas, Cass's background as a slave trader led to the removal of the name in 2020, being replaced 'for free' with the hopefully upstanding name of 18th Century statistician and Presbyterian Minister Thomas Bayes. One hopes for the best.

What we have not yet addressed here is the basis of the naming conventions. It will come of no surprise that the vast majority of donors have chosen to name the institution "'Name' School of Business" or similar. Of the 57 schools reviewed by Burch and Nanda, 42 are named in this manner. 15 are instead named "School of Management". Of the top 100 business schools in the 2021 Financial Times global rankings, only four of the top schools from the US are Schools of Management, the rest are business schools. It would be interesting to speak to donors about their decision-making criteria. Are they libertarian capitalists? Do they favor good management all around? Did they give this any thought at all? After all, what's in a name? Seemingly a fair amount. As Augier and March (2011, p.312) note:

> As more and more schools successfully solicited huge gifts from immensely rich individuals, more and more schools assumed the proper names of their benefactors and drifted toward the business, economic, and political prejudices that the donor embraced.

As one looks at other geographies, one sees different approaches. In the 2021 Financial Times ranking of European Business Schools, with the caveat that some schools are named in their domestic language, there is a much higher proportion, approximately 25%, that are called Schools of Management. Many of these are outside of the UK, featuring regularly in Scandinavia, Germany, in the Benelux and in France. As Cornuel, Thomas and Wood (2021) note in their commentary, the European culture and environment encourages more direct cooperation with government in order to address such issues as social inclusion, inequality, poverty and environmental sustainability and hence, helps to enhance human, social and economic progress, Because of these contextual and cultural differences there is both a discernable "European identity" and welcome diversity in European management models. Just as there is no common North American model, there is no common European management model. (Thomas, Lorange and Sheth 2013). That said, Europeans believe strongly in a balanced philosophy of management education in which important skills of analysis are nurtured alongside "softer" management skills of creativity, criticism and synthesis. This balanced approach seeks to produce managers who possess a sense of social responsibility as well as a moral authority to guide and lead others. Broadening out to look at the non-US or European schools in the 2021 Financial Times global rankings, it is notable that in India with the preponderance of the Institutes of Management, and also in China, a version of 'Schools of Management' dominates.

It is impossible to state categorically that these differences in naming conventions are the result of different concepts of how and where management education ought to be taught. That said, there has certainly been an ongoing debate between management educators in the U.S. and outside of the U.S. on what management is about, on whether sustainability is a proper subject, on the ethical responsibilities of managers. As we have seen, the debate in the U.S. is more capitalist and "business school" while the debate in Europe reflects the social democratic systems of

government and thus more "school of management". In other cases naming conventions have historical roots that change with the times. A telling example can be found with SGH in Poland. Founded in 1906 as the 'August Zielinski Private Trade Courses for Men', it was renamed as Szkoła Główna Handlowa (effectively Main School of Commerce) in 1933. After World War Two, it was renamed Szkoła Główna Planowania I Statystyki (Main School of Planning and Statistics) before being re-renamed SGH in 1991. In English, the institute is known as the Warsaw School of Economics. Clearly, politics had much to do with the naming conventions of schools.

Interestingly, Kociatkiewicz, Kostera and Zueva (2021), academics originally from Poland and Russia and now spread across France, Sweden, the UK and Poland, make a three-fold argument: they argue that capitalism is a ghost in the walls of the business school; that capitalism's ghostly nature prevents the business school from offering a curriculum that serves more than the growth of financial capital; and thirdly that the naming of capitalism is integral to the exorcism of its ghost and the creation of curriculum that engages with the social and environmental challenges of our time.

In addition to noting that there is a greater emphasis on 'Schools of Management' outside of the United States than within, it is also worth noting that with a number of exceptions, very few business schools outside of North America are named. Even in the UK, which always seems a hybrid between the United States and Europe, only Oxford Said, Cambridge Judge and Manchester Alliance come to mind. Continental Europe has a number of institutions that are named, but in most cases, the names arose from a founder or founding donor. Asia is largely similar although there are many private institutions or corporate funded institutions that do carry names.

Global Focus **Annual Research** Volume 1

Business Schools should be Schools of Management: An Evolutionary Perspective
Kai Peters and Howard Thomas
....

IN SUMMARY

In terms of curriculum, we have attempted to show how the original late 19th and early 20th century desire to train individuals as better managers, began as a relatively messy affair with no clear concept of what ought to be taught. Within the first few decades of the 20th century, a number of competing visions arose: courses aimed at specific industries, courses largely based on the humanities, and courses taking a quantitative, economics-based approach. Driven in part by the experience of the two World Wars, and hugely influenced by the post war interplay between think tanks like RAND, the cold war and individuals like Joseph McCarthy, and the Foundations, humanistic elements in the curriculum were exorcised as socialist, and a quantitative, capitalist, regulation-avoiding, free-market supporting vision of the role of business schools emerged.

The emergence of Business Week and Financial Times business school rankings accelerated this trend further. Hyper-competition in the management education landscape costs significant amounts of money. Schools were eager to receive donations in exchange for naming rights. These donations, culminating to date in the $300M donation by David Booth, a fund manager to the beacon of capitalistic business schools at the University of Chicago, embedded the capitalist vision further so that today only 4 of the top US schools are not named. Unsurprisingly, given that the donations came from extremely wealthy individuals, their philosophical, social and political views became dominant.

Outside of North America, the historical experience has been different. The view of the role of business has been different, whether because of social democracy or because of communism. There was no McCarthy / HUAC era. The role of donors and the bestowing of names did not materialise in the same way. However, there was a willingness among rectors and presidents of specialist universities for business and management, for example Paris Dauphine, WU in Vienna, Copenhagen Business School, St Gallen to "without exception embrace inter-, multi- and trans-disciplinary curricula and have strong engagement with practitioners and public agencies. (Cornuel et al, 2021) As a result, while the vast majority of institutions providing management education are named business schools across the world, a significant proportion, predominantly outside of North America are named Schools of Management.

The point we have tried to make in this short chapter is that it would be much better for all involved if 'business schools' were not called 'business schools' but were actually more broadly oriented 'schools of management', returning full circle to their original orientation. Not only would this be beneficial in the long run for managers in businesses who

need to understand more than micro and macro-economics and statistics by genuinely engaging with the society in which they are actors, it would also open up management education more widely to the not-for-profit and public sectors where management is also needed – probably more than ever.

Grey (2004) calls for managers to connect to a wider set of public duties than that of corporate performance alone, noting that this was the original vision of Joseph Wharton when he donated money for the Wharton School in the US in 1881, a vision of a school of management. We concur. It is not realistic to imagine the unravelling of over 100 years of development within the management education sphere – there is too much path dependency involved – but it is nevertheless possible for many schools around the world to take on and verbalise a broader vision. For example, Harney and Thomas's (2020) book contains a model of liberal management education developed at Singapore Management University (SMU) in which the more analytical, technological and specialised management aspects are balanced by a sound understanding of the wider world through studies in the humanities and social science. The Thomas et al (2023) study of the processes and actors involved in SMU's evolution of expands on this theme. Perhaps it is, however, realistic for a number of institutions, assuming they are not 'named' by a donor, to change their own branding in a similar manner. Being called a 'school of management' does not seem to have hurt those that are named as such. It is hard to imagine a downside. The upside seems self-evident to us.

Bibliography

Augier, M, and March, J.G., (2011) *The Roots, Rituals and Rhetorics of Change: North American Business Schools after the Second World War*, Stanford, CA: Stanford Business Books

Bennis, W.G., and O'Toole, J., (2005) How business schools lost their way, *Harvard Business Review* 83:5 96-104

Burch, T.R., and Nanda, V., (2005) What's in a Name? Hotelling's Valuation Principle and Business School Namings, *Journal of Business*, 78:4 1111-1136

Cornuel, E., Thomas, H., and Wood, M., (2021) Looking back and thinking forward. The 15th Anniversary Edition of *Global Focus*, Brussels: EFMD Publications

Donham, W.B. (1927) The social significance of business, *Harvard Business Review*, July

Donham, W.B. (1935) The failure of business leadership and the responsibility of universities. *Harvard Business Review*, 11: 418-435

Friedman, M., (1970) The social responsibility of business is to increase its profits. *New York Times Magazine* 33:30 122-125

Ghoshal, S., (2005) Bad Management Theories are Destroying Good Management Practice, *Academy of Management Learning and Education*, 4:1 75-91

Grey, C., (2004) Reinventing Business Schools: The Contribution of Critical Management Education, *Academy of Management Learning and Education*, 3:2 178-86

Harney, S., and Thomas, H., (2020) *The Liberal Arts and Management Education*, Cambridge UK: Cambridge University Press

Khurana, R., (2007) *From Higher Aims to Hired Hands: The Social Transformation of American Business Schools and the Unfulfilled Promise of Management as a Profession*, Princeton, NJ: Princeton University Press

Kociatkiewicz, J., Kostera, M, and Zueva, A, (2021) The ghost of capitalism: A guide to seeing, naming and exorcising the spectre haunting the business school, *Management Learning*, 1-21

Marshall, L., (1913) The College of Commerce and Administration of the University of Chicago, *Journal of Political Economy* 21:2: 97-110

Mintzberg, H., (2004) *Managers not MBAs: a Hard Look at the Soft Practice of Managing and Management Development*, San Francisco, CA: Berrett-Koehler

Mulligan, T., (1987) The two cultures in business education. *Academy of Management Review* 12:4 593-599

Parker, M., (2018) *Shut Down the Business School: What's Wrong with Management Education?* London: Pluto Press

Pettigrew, A., and Starkey, K., (2016) The Legitimacy and Impact of Business Schools – Key Issues and a Research Agenda, *Academy of Management Learning and Education*, 15:4, 649-664

Pfeffer, J., and Fong, C.T., (2002) The End of Business Schools? Less success than meets the eye. *Academy of Management Learning and Education* 1:1 78-95

Policano, A. (2005). What price rankings? *Biz Ed, an AACSB publication*, Sept/Oct

Starkey, K., and Thomas, H., (2019) What should Business Schools be for? *Global Focus*, 13:3, 40-45

Thomas, H., Lorange, P., and Sheth, J., (2013) *The Business School in the Twenty-First Century*, Cambridge, UK: Cambridge University Press

Thomas, H., Wilson, A., and Lee, M., (2023) *Creating a New Management University: tracking the Strategy of Singapore Management University 1997 – 2020*, Abingdon, UK: Routledge

Yogev, E., (2001) Corporate Hand in Academic Glove: The New Management's Struggle for Academic Recognition – The Case of the Harvard Group in the 1920's, *American Studies International*, 39, 1, pp 52-71

About the Authors

Kai Peters is Pro-Vice-Chancellor, Business and Law, at Coventry University, UK.

Howard Thomas is the Dean of Fellows at the British Academy of Management, Emeritus Professor at Singapore Management University and Senior Advisor at EFMD Global.

The Search for Meaning: BSIS and its Role in Promoting Business Schools' Societal Impact

MICHEL KALIKA AND ERIC CORNUEL

In a packed and admiring Amphitheatre, a professor delivers a magnificent lecture on the existence of God. The topics and arguments flow: according to Plato, God is both good and just ..., in the view of St Thomas Aquinas, faith and reason are compatible and reason helps us to access God ..., according to Nietzsche, God is dead ...

At the end of the lecture, a student asks the professor a question: "Do you, Professor, believe in God?

The professor answers in the usual manner: "according to Plato ..., according to Saint Thomas ..., according to Nietzsche ... etc."

To which the student replies by asking again: "I hear you, Professor, but, YOU, do YOU believe in God?"

And the professor, suddenly feeling uncomfortable and hesitant, answers: "Me? Do I believe in God? I don't know, I've never really thought about it!"

The exchanges between the professor and the student, could be likened to management research, which develops impressively coherent and intelligent arguments, while "thinking a lot", but without really tackling the most fundamental questions or developing convictions to inform decision-making.

As a matter of fact, the difficulty raised in our introduction goes beyond research questions to touch on the entire history of management education.

Bennis and O'Toole's[1] seminal article suggested that business schools had primarily evolved into academic institutions rather than advocates of new approaches for managers. In particular, they pointed out that business schools were much more focused on research than on the training and needs of managers: "Some of the research produced is excellent, but because so little of it is grounded in actual business practices, the focus of graduate business education has become increasingly circumscribed-and less and less relevant to practitioners."

This, of course, has a knock- on effect on business school research since the question of how to address the impact of research is generally answered in quantitative measures, league tables, of academic research output rather than more balanced measures of practical relevance and meaningful, managerial impact.Simply put, the value of research for all business school stakkeholders is often under emphasised.

The argument presented in this paper is based on the experience of the Business School Impact System (BSIS)[2] developed by the FNEGE and the EFMD over the last 10 years. Institutions participating in the BSIS, which has been used by nearly 70 business schools in 18 countries, have often expressed a need for new approaches to measuring the impact of the research they produce. It became apparent that BSIS was not only a tool for measuring impact, but also a way to generate value based on the research carried out by faculty for business school stakeholders, that is to say companies, governments, and society. Indeed, one of the main characteristics of BSIS is to express a holistic perspective of the impact of a business school.

DOI: 10.4324/9781003390633-4

Global Focus **Annual Research** Volume 1

The Search for Meaning: BSIS and its Role in Promoting Business Schools' Societal Impact
Michel Kalika and Eric Cornuel
....

THE EMERGENCE OF IMPACT IN MANAGEMENT EDUCATION

Business schools have two fundamental responsibilities. On the one hand, they have a responsibility to their students, whom they must prepare as best they can to develop careers that make a positive contribution to companies and are fulfilling for the students themselves. And on the other hand, a responsibility to employers, to whom they must provide the people capital and skills they need.

This basic observation reminds us of the obvious, namely the extent to which businesses and their developments occupy a fundamental place in the world of management education.

Impact and the search for meaningful impact are hot topics for both universities and business and management schools[3] even if it is not a new issue. Pettigrew & Starkey already took centre stage on the question of the legitimacy and impact of Business Schools[4]. The question of research impact is inextricably linked to that of the connection between research and teaching. This is because teaching, particularly in executive education, is how new knowledge is transformed into new managerial practices. The specific role of applied research is to be underlined, of course.

However, businesses have seen their work become focused on new themes; first of all CSR, and more recently ESG, the triple bottom line, and so on. It therefore seems logical that the very concept of impact itself is changing profoundly, especially as the increasing cost of research is leading to legitimate reflection on the proper allocation of resources in business schools.

Thus, both stakeholders and the media are increasingly questioning the purpose of the research conducted in schools. Is it only used to manage the careers of professors and to serve accreditation applications? What is the real influence of management research on managerial practice?

In order to effectively address the issue of the impact of management research and its measurement, a number of fundamental notions must first be clarified.

THE AMBIGUITY OF THE QUESTION OF "WHO IS IMPACTED" BY MANAGEMENT RESEARCH

The standard conception of research impact is usually based on bibliometric measures linked to the number of citations of articles, and the ranking of journals according to their impact score. These quantitative measures provide information about the impact of publications on the academic community, on colleagues, but totally omit the question of their impact on practitioners or society. Academic articles in the field of management are very rarely read by practitioners. It therefore appears that if academic impact is to be properly understood, it must be completed by the managerial and societal impact of the research.

THE IMPACT OF MANAGEMENT RESEARCH: AN AMBIGUOUS DEFINITION?

The definition of the impact of research often leads to confusion between inputs, i.e., resources allocated to research (budgets, recruitment of researchers), research activities (seminars, conferences, etc.), outputs (published articles), outcomes (readership, citations) and impacts, i.e., changes brought about by research in the behaviour of decision-makers and, more generally, in managerial practices. However, the definition of academic impact is generally limited to outputs and outcomes. This semantic confusion is obviously due to the ease with which metrics can be produced and the difficulty of measuring managerial and societal impact, which is often qualitative by nature.

The question is therefore how to measure the real impact of management research? The starting point is to redefine the purpose of management research and to recognise that the impact of research goes beyond publications.

REORIENTING RESEARCH TOWARDS MANAGERIAL AND SOCIETAL IMPACT RATHER THAN PUBLICATION

The remuneration and career progression systems of business schools result in many management researchers being more motivated by the search for stars and the 'impact factor' (the latter highlighting the ambiguity of the term impact) than by the real impact of their work on the management of organisations. For research developed in business schools to have a real influence on organisations, research objectives should therefore be reoriented towards managerial and societal impact[5] and not only towards publication metrics.

Impact assessment is inextricably linked to the incentive system, which must itself be consistent with the research objectives set by each business school.

Global Focus **Annual Research** Volume 1

The Search for Meaning: BSIS and its Role in Promoting Business Schools' Societal Impact
Michel Kalika and Eric Cornuel
....

Incentive systems should therefore be modified, by developing internal research evaluation systems, and by including new measures of managerial and societal impact.

If the business school aims to contribute to the sustainable development of society, it should adapt its incentive system and measurement tools. For example, it could evaluate research publications according to their relevance to the Sustainable Development Goals (SDGs)[6], or if the business school's mission is to contribute to the economic development of its territory, it will set incentives and impact measures that take into account the impact of its research on the work of local and regional businesses.

FACILITATING THE MANAGERIAL AND SOCIETAL IMPACT OF RESEARCH

This article argues that since management sciences have social practice as their raison d'être and condition for legitimacy, i.e., the activity of businesses, research in this field cannot be conceived as a closed system in which publications targeting academic audiences are evaluated according to academic criteria alone. In order to have an impact, research must also aim to both enlighten business actors and influence their practices.

However, the emphasis on this objective cannot hide the difficulties of the approach that it induces for research. In order to have a reasonable chance of generating impact, it is indispensable to influence the behaviour and practice of the principal actors, namely managers and businesses.

It is also essential to ask questions about the target audience for research, because such a reflection will lead to the infinitely more complex and fundamental question of the ways in which research has an impact: through what channels and through what social channels does research bring about social change?

This reflection, the need for which is eminent, is in its infancy. It has been the subject of reflection in developing the BSIS criteria, which has enabled us to set out simple elements as the basis for a more complete understanding of the way in which the managerial and societal impact of research can be expressed.

It should be emphasised that the targets of research can be individuals, organisations or society at large, and that the choice of one of these targets determines both the research strategy and its content. For example, the impact of research targeting individuals will obviously be through education; it will be blurred and delayed in undergraduate and postgraduate programmes; it will be immediate and more direct for management training. On the other hand, the target audiences deserve to be distinguished depending on their territory, since a business school may have research programmes in partnership with companies at regional, national or international level, therefore leading to different types of impact.

PROXIES FOR MEASURING AND/OR MAXIMISING THE MANAGERIAL AND SOCIETAL IMPACT OF RESEARCH

Measuring the impact of management research is a complex objective for which a methodology has not yet been officially developed.

The method that involves regularly asking managers or decision-makers about their perception of the impact of the research carried out is already quite frequently used, for example in surveys that ask which authors are the most influential. The disadvantage of these approaches is that they only target internationally known authors and neglect the vast majority of research that is conducted in business schools. They are difficult to generalise to research that is not produced by high-profile authors, as it is virtually impossible to ensure that the intended audience actually knows about the research in question outside the academic world.

Since it is impossible to observe the impact of research on businesses and, more generally, on organisations, it could be useful to deploy proxies that influence this impact.

We are aware that this approach involves shifting from measuring the impact of research to thinking about maximising that impact. However, listing the proxies of research appears to be a useful exercise insofar as it helps to take into account the fact that management research must, from the outset, take account of the fact that its raison d'être goes far beyond academic audiences. Moreover, it is a condition *sine qua non* as a first step towards a better understanding of the measurement of the impact of research.

We present six channels of dissemination of research results, taken from the perspective of generating impact on managers and organisations. It is important to emphasise that these channels are inseparable from and complement each other in creating and maximising the impact of research.

The first channel is teaching. Research should feed into the courses taken by undergraduate and postgraduate students: the messages, cases and concepts shared with them will influence their behaviour in business and more generally in society. It goes without saying that this impact is deferred since students are not yet working, except during internships, assignments and work-study programmes, such as apprenticeships. However, in the case of Executive Education courses and seminars, whether degree programmes or in-company programmes, the effect can be immediate.

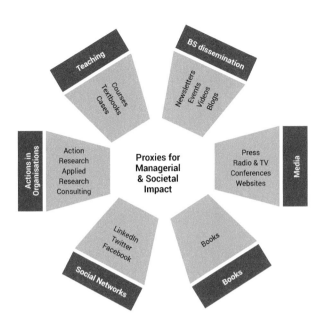

Figure 1 Proxies for Managerial & Societal Impact

Course books and case studies produced by professors are powerful means of disseminating research results in business school networks. For example, CEIBS and IMD are examples of institutions where professors publish a large number of cases and generate international impact.

The second channel of dissemination is the business school's own media resources. Some schools have created journals, research bulletins for managers, researcher-manager events, videos presenting their publications or even blogs. For example, FGV EAESP has created its own journal to disseminate the results of its professors' research using easily understandable managerial language.

The third channel is the mainstream and professional media: interviews, press, radio and TV appearances of professors, participation in professional conferences and videos of professors on online sites are all opportunities for impact. The University of Ljubljana is an example of the strong presence of its professors in the local media.

The fourth channel is books or book chapters, which are known to be more widely read by managers than academic articles. Bocconi SDA has established a reputation as a business school whose professors publish many books specifically for managers.

The fifth channel is social media, which is very popular with journalists, who are likely to relay professors' messages. Social media is also popular with many practitioners. LinkedIn, Twitter and Facebook are all examples of ways of relaying the information mentioned above.

The sixth channel is action research (or intervention research), in which researchers carry out transformative work in companies and organisations. This type of research has a powerful and direct impact on the organisation. The same applies to applied research or consultancy activities carried out by professors.

CONCLUSION

The inspiration for this article has been based on two main observations:

- Firstly, the world of business has undergone a fundamental upheaval in the last 20 years with the emergence of the theme of the social role of the company, as evidenced by the emphasis placed on CSR, ESG, sustainability, etc. This new context creates an expectation that management research should cover topics that go beyond the field of business.

- Secondly, this new context creates a renewed demand on managers, who are required not only to be ready to account for their actions, but also be responsive and autonomous to cope with the accelerated pace of business. One of the consequences of this double movement is that business schools now more often remain in touch with managers throughout their professional lives (in particular, through executive programmes), and that managers express a renewed need and expectation for research to be relevant to them, and therefore help them take decisions and initiatives.

The reinforced affirmation of the need for management research to take into account both the external environment of the company and its own relevance, not only for academics but especially for managers, underlines the importance of the impact of management research.

The measurement of the impact of management research, in academic terms, is undergoing constant progress, as evidenced, for example, by the continued development of impact factor indices. This is also aligned with the mission of the EFMD and its historical focus on social responsibility. It is also coherent with the standards and criteria of accreditation as guarantors of the quality of business schools.

This article highlights the importance of developing measures of the impact of management research that take into account its managerial and social aspects. It highlights the immense challenges, which are still poorly taken into account in the current state of this approach: evaluations that are at best only declarative, the need to find methodologies that are not limited to the quantitative but take into account the qualitative aspects (in particular the narratives that tell the true story of the impact of management research), and the need to take into account that impact is not immediate and that its benefits may be deferred, etc.

Finally, this article resonates with the work of Michel Foucault who argued that elements of knowledge relating to only part of the field to be studied, but leading to a practice, enable a *Will to Knowledge*[7] to be developed, which puts one in a position to elaborate a more thorough approach.

From this perspective, we have emphasised the importance of maximising societal and managerial impact (while fully recognising that this is only a very fragmented aspect of the wider impact issue). By detailing six channels of impact maximisation, we contribute to one of the many aspects of this question. But more importantly, by initiating *The Will to Knowledge*, we hope to induce a process that will allow a more comprehensive approach to the impact of management research to be developed over time.

Footnotes

[1] Bennis WG, O'Toole J *How business schools have lost their way* - , 2005

[2] Financial, educational, business development, intellectual, regional ecosystem, societal and image impact.

[3] See for example the recent book: Haley, U.C. (2021). *Impact and the Management Researcher*. Routledge.

[4] Pettigrew, A., & Starkey, K. (2016). From the guest editors: The legitimacy and impact of business schools—Key issues and a research agenda. *Academy of Management Learning & Education, 15*(4), 649-664.

[5] https://www.rrbm.network

[6] https://linkprotect.cudasvc.com/url?a=https%3a%2f%2frsmmetrics.nl%2fsustainable-development-goals%2ftriple-crown-sdg&c=E,1,W17W-glyiu9LwD3FXipqyKjDqwzMLb-eazupMFblmetiQ5ZB7GUyZgu21nsp2DDL17jP8FGeGaKPhElHDLCCBpKgBAHQM9NNxFtfp0GCszUllg,,&typo=1

[7] Michel Foucault, *The History of Sexuality: 1: The Will to Knowledge* Paperback −1998 Robert Hurley (Translator)

About the Authors

Michel Kalika is Founder and Senior advisor, BSIS at EFMD Global, and President at Business Science Institute.

Eric Cornuel is President, EFMD Global.

What Topics Should Business School Research Focus on?

ANNE S. TSUI, MARY JO BITNER AND SERGUEI NETESSINE

Insights from 123 Award-winning Responsible Research Projects

A WORLD IN NEED OF SCIENCE-BASED SOLUTIONS

In recent years, there is an active conversation within the business research community of the need to give more research attention to the grand challenges of the world. There is also an increasing awareness, which became particularly salient as the world endures the COVID-19 pandemic, of the importance of science-based knowledge or solutions to tackle many life-threatening or existential crises in both developed and developing worlds. As articulated by the United Nations Global Compact through the seventeen Sustainable Development Goals,[2] business firms are powerful instruments for solving most of these grand challenges, alongside government and non-profit agencies. At the same time, young scholars, especially the millennials and the generation Z, are eager to contribute to a better world by working on research that matters. In response to the challenges of the time, many business and management journals are beginning to welcome problem-inspired research, pivoting away from literature-motivated research. Furthermore, the accreditation agencies of business schools, such as AACSB and EFMD, have introduced new standards to encourage attention to the societal impact of the schools' research, education, and outreach programmes. But the pace of change toward problem-solving business research is very slow. Without a substantial infusion of science-based new knowledge, business school curricula and business education will continue to fail in meeting the needs of the changed and changing world.[3]

The Responsible Research in Business and Management network (www.rrbm.network), founded in early 2015 by 24 leading scholars (including the three authors of this paper) in the core business disciplines and from ten countries, serves as a catalyst to encourage, recognise, and stimulate research that produces both credible and useful knowledge. The former refers to research findings that are reliable,

trustworthy, and replicable, which is necessary to solve the "credibility or replication crisis". The latter refers to research findings that are related to important problems in the real world with potential applications that can improve the life of stakeholders (such as workers, consumers, and communities), beyond the financial return to the shareholders. This focus on usefulness is to solve the "relevance" or "research-practice gap" problem, a great concern to many business scholars for almost three decades.

Business schools were originally founded to solve the needs of society including efficient productions of goods and services that societies need. Over time, this attention to the needs of society has shifted to maximizing shareholder returns. Correspondingly, there was much less attention to life-improving outcomes for stakeholders beyond shareholders in business research. Analyses of published articles in the leading management journals have found more than 80% to focus on the financial or economic outcomes valued by owners or top managers and less than 20% on outcomes valuable to other stakeholders like employees, customers, or society.[4] Some of the consequences of the narrow pursuit of maximizing shareholder value are resource depletion, environmental degradation, global economic inequality, and climate change – all of which have become some of the grand challenges of our time. The struggle with the COVID-19 pandemic added oil to the fire. It is so much more urgent for the scientific communities, natural and social, to offer evidence-based solutions to address the wicked problems causing suffering for most of humanity. Business schools and business scholars have a great opportunity and a grave responsibility to contribute to creating and disseminating science-based knowledge to a world in need, highlighting the role of businesses in addressing the grand challenges such as the Sustainable Development Goals.

DOI: 10.4324/9781003390633-5

WHAT TOPICS SHOULD BUSINESS RESEARCH FOCUS ON?

Responsible research calls for a more balanced attention to outcomes important to all stakeholders. Fortunately, in response to society's expectations, even among for-profit corporations, there is a growing awareness that something must be done differently to realign business with the rapidly changing global economic context and to avert the grave condition of our future if the grand challenges are not addressed in a timely fashion. This new realization is evident in the redefinition of "Corporate Purpose" by the Business Roundtable (members are CEOs of leading US companies) on August 19, 2019.[5] The signatories of this statement, 181 CEOs, "commit to lead their companies for the benefit of all stakeholders—customers, employees, suppliers, communities, and shareholders". The 2022 World Economic Forum Global Risk report[6] identifies social cohesion erosion, livelihood crises, mental health deterioration, debt crisis, cybersecurity failures, digital inequality, and backlash against science as the most concerning problems in the world today and in the near future.

What do business scholars concerned with relevance consider to be topics of importance? Through a Delphi study, the RRBM "position paper"[7] identifies five topics that received the greatest assent. These topics align well with the United Nations' Sustainable Development Goals.

1. Understanding the broader impact of firms on and their roles in society, beyond the creation of shareholder value.
2. Understanding the changing nature of work and the workforce, as well as the changing nature of consumers and their role in co-creating value.
3. Examining the social sustainability of business organisations, including their impact on the health and well-being of employees, customers, and community.
4. Enhancing environmental sustainability, managing the use of natural resources, and reducing negative environmental impact.
5. Alleviating poverty, creating greater prosperity, and reducing economic inequality, both locally and globally.

In the face of these existential challenges affecting developed and developing economies alike, research in business schools cannot and must not continue with "business as usual". Grand challenges by nature are big, complex, and wicked for which solutions cannot be easily identified. It is understandable, though disappointing, that most business researchers, like part of the society, have ignored the problem of global warming and climate change—which is not a meterological problem but a business problem. There has been limited research on how business activities have contributed to global warming and on the impact of global warming on lives around the world now and in the future. COVID-19 provided another wake-up call by revealing the gross inequity in public health, both within and across countries. The pandemic led to economic disruptions by large and small businesses, displacing millions of workers, and weakening the global supply chain. With over ten thousand business schools worldwide and thousands of articles published per year, we should be able to expect more science-based solutions to pressing challenges than have been offered to the public. A recent essay in AACSB Insights reported a study of how business schools worldwide have paid little attention to the 17 SDGs since 2015.[8] A few schools have integrated the SDGs into their teaching and research, but the overall conclusion is that the attention is much less than expected. Even a year ago, when we asked a group of participants at a webinar how many of them have heard of the SDGs, the response disappointed us.

However, we can be optimistic that many business schools and scholars are beginning to engage in deep reflection, along with an awakening to our duty as responsible social scientists. The call for responsible research by the RRBM network is long overdue. Responsible research is no more difficult or easy than traditional research. The work of the three 2019 Nobel laureates in Economic Science provide a good example of how a complex problem like poverty can be studied by breaking it down into manageable research questions. They focused primarily on public health, early childhood education, and agriculture. By using Randomised Controlled Trials (RCT), with repeated testing (replications) of interventions (e.g., ways to reduce teacher and nurse absencies, to incentivise farmers to use pesticides), their research yielded great impact: five million Indian children benefited from remedial teaching; many countries increased their spending on preventative health care, and great improvements were realised in agricultural yield. The RCT method is not restricted to medical or economic research. Business researchers have used field experimentation for many decades.

Global Focus **Annual Research** Volume 1

What Topics Should Business School Research Focus on?
Anne S. Tsui, Mary Jo Bitner and Serguei Netessine

THE RESPONSIBLE RESEARCH AWARD

To encourage more attention to tackle the research topics that are of importance to stakeholders beyond shareholders, RRBM supported the creation of a Responsible Research Award in three disciplines: management, marketing, and operations management.[9] The purpose of this annual award is to identify and recognise research that exemplies the seven principles of responsible research.[10] Principle 1 is to support the basic goal of science, that scientific work is to serve society. Principles 2 to 4 are to provide guidelines on designing research that will enhance the credibility of the findings. Principles 5 to 7 offer various ways to include stakeholders in the research process to improve the relevance of the research for them and to ensure the discoveries will provide actionable and beneficial ideas. These three awards are managed by the three sponsoring disciplinary societies with open nominations of research published in the previous one to five years. The nominations go through a rigorous review process and are judged by highly accomplished scholars. In the case of management, the nominations are also evaluated by a team of executives who assess the relevance of the topics for practice or policy. The award has been given for four years in management (2018-2021), three years in marketing (2020-2022), and three years in Operations Management (2019-2021).[11] A total of 108 articles (60 in management, 35 in marketing, and 13 in operations management) and 15 books (14 in Management and one in Marketing) have won this award to date. We analysed these research projects to identify the major research themes, the primary stakeholders who may potentially benefit from the research, and the methods the authors used to disseminate their work as described in the nomination letters – so that the findings can reach the communities of practice. We are pleased to report the major insights from these outstanding research projects, first the 108 research articles and then the 15 research books.

RESEARCH THEMES AMONG THE 108 AWARD WINNING RESEARCH ARTICLES

Table 1 shows the major themes we identified in the 108 winning articles, mapped onto the 17 sustainable development goals. With one exception, Organisational Outcomes, each of the major themes identified in the papers can be linked to multiple SDGs, as indicated by the relevant SDG numbers in the parentheses in column one of Table 1.[12]

Major Themes (e.g., relevant SDGs)	Management	Marketing	Operations Management	Total	%
	60 (100%)	35 (100%)	13 (100%)	108	100%
Well-Being (e.g., SDG 1, 2, 3, 8)	17 (28%)	14 (40%)	6 (46%)	37	34%
Justice/ Equity (e.g., SDG 5, 10)	13 (22%)	6 (17%)	4 (31%)	23	21%
Sustainability (e.g., SDG 6, 7, 12, 13)	12 (20%)	7 (20%)	1 (8%)	20	19%
Institutions/ Infrastructure (e.g., SDG 9, 11, 16)	7 (12%)	6 (17%)	2 (15%)	15	14%
Organisational Outcomes	11 (18%)	2 (6%)	0 (0%)	13	12%

Table 1 Major Themes (Outcomes) in the 108 Award Winning Articles

Well-Being

Well-Being is the largest theme, representing 34% of all awards, across disciplines. Within marketing and operations management, the percentage is even higher at 40% and 46%. Well-Being focuses on individuals as well as communities and spans different types of well-being including health, financial, social, and disaster recovery.

The health sub-theme includes physical health, emotional health, identity, and well-being of individual workers, consumers, and communities. For example, one marketing award-winning paper studied over-the-counter drug use and potential overdosing by consumers. Through five empirical studies the authors identified communication interventions that would help to avoid unintentional overdosing by consumers (Caitlin, Pechmann, & Brass, 2015). Several other marketing award-winners focused on promoting healthy food choices. For example, Berry et al. (2019) explored the paradox of including calorie counts on menus and found that showing calories does not necessarily lead to lower calorie menu item choices.

Global Focus **Annual Research** Volume 1

What Topics Should Business School Research Focus on?
Anne S. Tsui, Mary Jo Bitner and Serguei Netessine
··················

A management award-winning study focused on health of patients with rare diseases. The authors (Kucukkeles, Ben-Menahem & von Krogh, 2019) focused on a practice known as drug repurposing or drug repositioning. This study identifies the ways in which nonprofit actors can propel drug repurposing by engaging patients in the drug development process, creating platforms and communities for knowledge exchange among diverse stakeholders. This study offers valuable knowledge on the comparative efficacy of alternative organisational arrangements such as social entrepreneurship for tackling societal challenges.

Other award-winners studied social well-being of communities and financial/economic well-being of vulnerable groups. In one ethnographic marketing study, the researchers focused on community recovery and well-being following a series of earthquakes. The research tracked the development and effectiveness of an alternative market structure – namely "time banks". Time banks facilitate and track the exchange of services among community members through time currencies earned by individuals who provide skills or services to a community member and in turn have the opportunity to use their time currency in exchange for an unrelated service from another community member. This innovative exchange structure promoted adaptive capacities and fostered resiliency within the community as it restructured following the disasters (Ozanne & Ozanne, 2016). Another award-winner focused on underserved consumers living in geographic bank deserts, identifying communication and organisational strategies for banks entering those markets that would increase access to banking services (financial well-being) for vulnerable consumers (Mende et al., 2019)

A management award-winning paper (Shepherd & Williams, 2014) studied how local people organised compassion ventures to alleviate the suffering of victims after major natural disasters. Another paper (Ballesteros, Useem & Wry, 2017) found regions hit by natural disasters

recovered much faster when they received substantial aid from firms with local operations than from other sources. These studies show how business and entrepreneurship can directly contribute to citizen well-being when disasters strike.

In operations management, there are many papers focusing directly on health. For instance, Jonasson et al. (2017) demonstrates how to achieve improvements in HIV Early Infant Diagnosis in Sub-Saharan Africa by improving assignment of clinics to laboratories and the allocation of capacity across laboratories. While many papers in operations management directly concern the healthcare industry, there are also papers studying a different angle of well-being such as safety. Ibanez and Toffel (2020) studied outcomes of thousands of food safety inspections and found that inspectors were affected by the inspection outcomes at their prior-inspected establishment. Choudhary et al. (forthcoming) focuses on increasing safety of drivers using simple behavioral nudges.

Justice/Equity

The justice/equity theme represents 21% of all award winners and includes papers that focus on social, economic, gender, and race equity. Among marketing award-winners, several papers focused on advancing racial equity in marketing and business practices. For example, one study (Bone, Christensen, & Williams, 2014) observed minority business customers' access to bank loans, demonstrating the negative effects on self-concept of restricted choice because of systemic biases. The research has had long-lasting impact on banking practices and public policy related to minority business loans. Among operations management papers, Ata et al. (2017) demonstrate feasibility of reducing geographic disparity among kidney transplant patients using private jets to increase geography for matching. As another example, Cui et al. (2020) demonstrate how reviews can reduce racial discrimination in the sharing economy using experiments on AirBnB.

A management award winner (Liu, et al., 2020) studied bias in hiring. The authors identified an easy to implement intervention−−grouping job candidates into different categories to nudge decision makers to choose more diverse candidates without lowering the average competence of the selected candidates. This research provides a solution that contributes both to better business and to a better world. Another study (Hideg, et al., 2018) focused on the negative effect of long maternity leave on women's career advancement in the context of Canadian maternity leave policies. They found that when corporate programmes kept the women engaged in the workplace during the long leave, the women were less likely to incur negative career consequences.

Global Focus **Annual Research** Volume 1

What Topics Should Business School Research Focus on?
Anne S. Tsui, Mary Jo Bitner and Serguei Netessine
....

Sustainability

The sustainability theme, representing 19% of all award winners includes papers on climate change, ESG themes, social sustainability, natural resources, and responsible production and consumption. The emphasis is on business practices and individual behaviors that promote innovation in the preservation of resources.

Environmental (climate and ESG) topics were prominent in the management discipline award-winners. For example, a 2021 winner of the award (Rousseau, Berrone & Gelabert 2019) focused on SDG#11 which is about making cities inclusive, safe, resilient, and sustainable. The authors explored how the density of local environmental nonprofit organisations (LENOs) promotes city sustainability. Using a panel dataset of 100 U.S. metropolitan statistical areas (MSAs) over 12 years, they discovered that a higher density of LENOs is associated with a reduction in toxic contamination and an increase in the adoption of voluntary environmental standards at the city level. The study also identified some conditions when the effects of LENOs are stronger or weaker. The study results offer important implications for urban city designers and policy makers

In marketing, the dominant sustainability focus was on responsible consumption and responsible product disposition. For example, one paper (Winterich, Nenkov, & Gonzales, 2019) focused on communication and positioning messages related to recycled products found that consumers are more likely to recycle when they are told specifically how the recycled products will be transformed into new products. Another award-winning paper studied messaging approaches that retailers can use to increase the purchase of unattractive, but perfectly good, produce products (Grewal et al., 2019). Often these unattractive or imperfect produce items are not offered at all, or they are thrown out, increasing food waste. Through a series of experiments, including one in the field, the researchers were able to show that various messaging strategies which increase consumer self-esteem led to increased purchase of unattractive produce.

Institutions/Infrastructure

The Institutions/Infrastructure theme, representing 14% of all award winners, included research on business practices and individual actions that promote more responsible approaches by institutions (e.g., professions or government) and infrastructure (e.g., technology) in ways that will benefit society. Among the management award winners, there was a significant focus on specific professions such as adopting green chemistry practices (Howard-Grenville, et al., 2017) in the chemical profession, stigmatization of the medical profession by patients and citizens (Wang, Raynard, & Greenwood, 2020), or commercialization of religious organisations (Yue, Wang & Yang, 2019).

In marketing, most papers within this theme emphasised ethics and transparency in technology and social media, focusing on topics such as the effects of default privacy and security settings on trust and transparency when consumers are asked to share information online (Walker, 2016) and the ethics and privacy implications of mothers sharing children's information online (Fox & Hoy 2019).

Examples in Operations Management include Gui et al. (2016) which develops cost allocation mechanisms that induce participation in large collection and recycling network systems to maximise cost efficiency and collections. Another example is Zhang et al. (2020) which analyses a resource allocation problem faced by medical surplus recovery organisations which recover medical surplus products to fulfill the needs of underserved healthcare facilities in developing countries.

Organisational Outcomes

This is the smallest theme, representing 12% of all award winners. Four of these papers are in management, with two in marketing and none in operations management. These papers focused on strategies aimed at business success such as a long-term orientation (Flammer & Bansal, 2017), or personal initiative training for entrepreneurial success in Africa (Campo, et al., 2017). In marketing, papers falling within this theme focused on increasing organisational success of nonprofit organisations through strategies that enhance donations (Yin, Li & Singh, 2020; Fajardo, Townsend, & Bolander, 2018).

STAKEHOLDERS WHO MAY BENEFIT FROM THE RESEARCH

Award-winning papers are expected to benefit stakeholders beyond increasing financial returns to firms and shareholders. We analysed which stakeholders may potentially benefit from the findings of the 108 award-winning research projects.

Table 2 illustrates the wide range of stakeholders who are the primary beneficiaries of the award-winning research, and they logically differ across the three disciplines. Employees/workers are the most frequent stakeholder beneficiary of management award winning projects (32% of management papers) while consumers/customers are the most common stakeholder beneficiary for marketing award winners (46%). Society is the most frequent group for operations management (38%); it is the second largest for management (27%) and marketing (28%). The second most common stakeholder group for Operations Management is consumers/customers (31%). Combining all three disciplines, society is the major stakeholder beneficiary (38%), then consumers/customers (19%) and employees/workers (18%). Including patients in the consumers/customers group increases that beneficiary group to 25% of the total.

Global Focus **Annual Research** Volume 1

What Topics Should Business School Research Focus on?
Anne S. Tsui, Mary Jo Bitner and Serguei Netessine

A few studies focused on multiple stakeholders. For example, a study on a social enterprise (Smith & Besharov, 2019) has potential benefits for both employees and society. We found 14 of the 108 articles (13%) have potential benefits for two or more stakeholders. This is a major departure from the past with a major shareholder-benefiting orientation, i.e., executives, owners, or shareholders.

RESEARCH THEMES AND BENEFITING STAKEHOLDERS OF THE 15 AWARD WINNING RESEARCH BOOKS

The main themes of the research books are broad in nature. Ten of the 15 research books are about building stronger institutions such as reimagining capitalism to focus on purpose, shared values, and long-term solutions to wicked problems (Henderson, 2020) or building sustainable and scalable enterprises at the bottom of the pyramid to reduce poverty (London, 2016). Other examples include using multistakeholder partnerships to solve wicked problems (Gray & Purdy, 2018), using the B Corps to create better business (Marquis, 2020), identifying the contribution of educated Russian immigrants to innovation and the US economy (Puffer, McCarthy & Satinsky, 2018). While the primary theme in these books is about strong institutions, the secondary themes are for these institutions to improve the social justice and well-being of different stakeholders of the world.

In addition, three books focus on justice issues and two books on sustainability. For example, Johnson and collaborators (2019) published an edited volume of original research based on the premise that markets should be, but are not, equitable and just. The collection presents research by scholars in the interdisciplinary and global Race in the Marketplace Network that seeks to codify and advance understanding and solutions related to race and its intersecting socio-political constructs (e.g., class, gender, ethnicity, religion, and sexuality) in a variety of marketplace settings. Thomas and Hendrick-Wong (2019) use case studies to illustrate how access to vital networks for economic opportunities can be a way to narrow the gap between the wealthy and the poor. Hoffman (2015) examines crucial questions about the research on climate change, including why people reject scientific consensuses and why climate change is a part of culture wars in politics.

Given the broad foci of the books, the main stakeholder benefiting from these ideas is the people in our societies. A second stakeholder is marginalised populations such as the people at the bottom of the pyramid, racial minorities, or immigrants. Other beneficiaries include employees and business organisations.

Primary Stakeholder Beneficiaries	Specific beneficiary groups	No. (%) of Management articles	No. (%) of Marketing articles	No. (%) of OM articles	Total No. (%) of articles
		60 (100%)	35 (100%)	13 (100%)	108 (100%)
Society	Citizens, children, communities	16 (27%)	10 (28%)	5 (38%)	41 (38%)
Consumers/Customers	Poor/vulnerable, minority, entrepreneurs, technology users, online/retail store, bank, or food shoppers	0	16 (46%)	4 (31%)	20 (19%)
Employees/workers	Women, minority, transgender, supply chain, independent contractors, job applicants	19 (32%)	0	0	19 (18%)
Patients	Minority patients, rare disease, terminal, or cancer patients, pharmaceutical customers	3 (5%)	4 (11%)	1 (8%)	8 (7%)
Firms	Large firms, shareholders, nonprofits	5 (8%)	2 (6%)	0	7 (6%)
Entrepreneurs	Small businesses, women, technology	6 (10%)	0	0	6 (6%)
Non-business organisations	Religious, education	2 (3%)	1 (3%)	0	3 (3%)
Government and society	Regulators, investors, citizens	2 (3%)	2 (6%)	0	4 (4%)
Multiple stakeholders	Firms and employees, firms and society, employees and society	7 (12%)	0	3 (23%)	10 (9%)

Table 2 Stakeholder-Beneficiaries of 108 Award Winning Studies

Global Focus **Annual Research** Volume 1

What Topics Should Business School Research Focus on?
Anne S. Tsui, Mary Jo Bitner and Serguei Netessine

....

DISSEMINATION BEYOND THE ACADEMIC RESEARCH COMMUNITY

Based on RRBM principles, responsible research should have impact beyond the academic research community. While publication in leading academic journals and citations by other academics are important, they do not tell the story of actual impact on practice, policy, or society. To illustrate practical impact, academic research findings and implications should be disseminated to relevant stakeholder groups, such as students, government, policymakers, and media. Across the 108 award-winning papers a wide variety of dissemination methods were mentioned in the nomination letters, with many papers using multiple methods. Our analysis identified nine methods being used by these authors. They include, in descending order of the frequency with which they were utilised, (1) articles in practitioner outlets such as the *Harvard Business Review*, (2) presentation to organisational leaders or policy makers, (3) coverage by media, (4) presentation at practitioner conferences or events, (5) presence in social media and online platforms, (6) sharing with students in the classroom, (7) consultation or training projects with organisations or policy makers, (8) publicity through university media groups, and (9) books or white papers.

The most common media coverage in print, radio and TV included such outlets as *The New York Times*, *Wall Street Journal*, Bloomberg, *Forbes*, the *Financial Times*, *The Economist*, *Fast Company*, The Conversation, CNN, Huffington Post, American Banker, and many national newspapers in countries including Australia, China, France, Japan, the Netherlands, and the U.K. Other media included podcasts, YouTube, TedX, Twitter and Linked In. Presentations to organisational leaders and policy makers were made to the FDA, Consumer Financial Protection Bureau, U.S. Congressional committees, the World Bank, Asian Development Bank, and practitioner conferences such as the World Economic Forum.

A very important and easy approach to dissemination is through classrooms that educate students on the research findings and societal implications. Many of the award-winning research papers have also been adopted by faculty not associated with the original research team as required reading in their PhD seminars and MBA classrooms. One paper has become standard reading in business ethics courses worldwide. Finally, researchers frequently consult with partner companies and others to implement the research or develop training related to the research within organisations and government.

Some authors found unique ways to disseminate their research to non-academic communities, government, classroom, and business stakeholders. For example, one of the marketing award winners studied community outcomes (e.g., consumption opportunities, diversity, and interaction across groups) of gentrification and developed a film that illustrates the research findings and their societal implications. The film was shared with scholars, activists, community members, businesspeople, community developers, economists, public school teachers, real estate professionals, government officials and more (Grier & Perry, 2018). One management research team collaborated with Google to develop a 9-week training programme to help Asian employees to enhance their communication skills (Lu, Nisbett, & Morris, 2020). Another team informed the US Senate's S.230 hearings in October 2020. Later, the founder of Reddit contacted the authors to form a major collaboration with Sentropy (www.sentropy.com) to use AI tools to tackle the problems their research project revealed (Kitchens, Johnson, & Gray, 2020). The Communication Workers of America labor union is using the findings of an award-winning project to fight against hedge funds targeting AT&T (DesJardine, Marti, & Durand, 2021).

The dissemination methods for books are largely similar to those of articles. The book nomination letters describe numerous invitations to present the work at practitioner conferences or to various groups of policy makers and organisational leaders. Media coverage has involved a variety of well-known, geographically and professionally diverse outlets for print, audio, and video. Additional exposure for some books came through inclusion in recommended reading or book award lists, such as The Financial Times Top Business Books, Social Change Innovators Recommended Reads, FT & McKinsey Business Books of the Year, and Porchlight Business Books of the Year, among others. As with articles, several books (or cases developed from them) have been adopted for use in teaching across multiple universities. The Johnson, et al (2019) book is notable for its open-access availability and high download rate through the publisher's (Springer's) Black Lives Matter campaign.

BACKGROUND OF THE AWARD-WINNING AUTHORS

Lastly, we found encouraging diversity in the background of the authors of these award-winning research projects. We focused on the first authors since they are the intellectual leaders of these projects, reflected in the order of authorship in the three disciplines. Among the authors of the 108 research articles, 46% are female and 54% male. In terms of position rank, 44% of them are assistant professors, 22% associate and 29% full professors. The remaining are doctoral students and postdocs (5%). Most of them work in universities in the U.S. (71%) and 29% of them work in 12 other countries. Among the first authors of the 15 books, only three are female, and all of them are full professors. Ten of the 15 books were singled authored while only four of the 108 articles were single-authored.

Global Focus **Annual Research** Volume 1

What Topics Should Business School Research Focus on?
Anne S. Tsui, Mary Jo Bitner and Serguei Netessine
....

THE GRAND CHALLENGE FOR BUSINESS SCHOOLS: TO BE THE NORTH STAR FOR SCIENCE IN SERVICE TO SOCIETY

We hope our analysis of the 123 award-winning research projects in responsible research and the implications we drew have provided a promising answer to the question of our paper title "What topics should business school research focus on?" These award-winning papers cover a wide range of topics that relate to many of the Sustainable Development Goals and other grand challenges of the world. Reporting on the findings of these projects energised us and gave us much hope that business research has great potential to offer valuable knowledge to inform life-improving business practices and government policies. The primary focus on well-being and social justice with potential benefit to employees and communities will pay dividends for businesses as well. Healthy and happy citizens are also creative and productive employees. Responsible business research can create a win-win-win condition for employees (including both managers and workers), consumers, communities (including citizens and especially marginalised populations), and employers (including both suppliers and buyers). By focusing on RRBM's Principle 1 of "Science in service to society", business researchers can be the guiding light for businesses, non-profits, and government through delivering credible and useful knowledge.

While most of the award-winning projects offer actionable ideas, relatively few used field experiments to test specific interventions. We encourage greater use of the RCT method – randomised controlled trials – as the three 2019 Economic Science Nobel laureates did, to test interventions aimed at benefiting society and alleviating suffering through improving business practices. Experiments on ideas to reduce poverty, inequality, and discrimination, or to increase justice in resource allocation, education, healthcare, or shared prosperity can be conducted in organisations, societies, and even nation states. Such research may require multi-party collaboration involving businesses, NGOs, government agencies and researchers. Greater attention to and publication of replications also are necessary to make sure the conclusions are robust, and the risk of wrongful conclusion is minimised.

Beyond the practical wisdom of managers and policymakers, the world needs science-based actionable knowledge. Can business research become a guiding light by discovering and disseminating solutions to many wicked problems facing humanity? We believe it can. Business researchers must rise to the challenge of becoming a positive force for good in this troubled world.

Footnotes

[1] The three authors contributed equally to the work in this article. We thank Juliane Iannarelli for her assistance with the analysis of the management articles.

[2] https://sdgs.un.org/goals

[3] The challenges of business schools in the twenty-first century are well discussed in the book by Howard Thomas, Peter Lorange and Jagdish Sheth, 2013 by Cambridge University Press.

[4] Walsh, Weber & Margolis, in **Journal of Management**, 2003; Tsui & Jia, in **Management and Organisation Review**, 2013.

[5] https://www.businessroundtable.org/business-roundtable-redefines-the-purpose-of-a-corporation-to-promote-an-economy-that-serves-all-americans

[6] https://www.weforum.org/reports/global-risks-report-2022/digest

[7] https://www.rrbm.network/position-paper/

[8] https://www.aacsb.edu/insights/articles/2022/03/how-are-business-schools-engaging-in-the-sdgs

[9] The sponsors of these three awards are The Academy of Management Fellows, the American Marketing Association, and the Manufacturing and Service Operations Management Society, respectively.

[10] https://www.rrbm.network/executive-briefing/eb-principles/

[11] We will not offer a Reference list in this essay. You can find all the award-winning papers and books on the RRBM Awards page: www.rrbm.network/taking-action/awards

[12] Well-Being is tied to four of the seventeen SDGs: No Poverty (1), Zero Hunger (2), Good Health and Well-Being (3), and Decent Work and Economic Growth (8). Justice/Equity is tied to two of the SDGs: Gender Equality (5), and Reduced Inequalities (10). Sustainability is tied four of the SDGs: Clean Water and Sanitation (6), Affordable and Clean Energy (7), Responsible Consumption and Production (12), and Climate Action (13). Institutions/Infrastructure is tied to three SDGs: Industry Innovation and Infrastructure (9), Sustainable Cities and Communities (11), and Peace, Justice and Strong Institutions (16).

About the Authors

Anne S. Tsui is Motorola Professor International Management Emerita at the W.P. Carey School of Business, Arizona State University, USA.

Mary Jo Bitner is Professor Marketing Emerita at W.P. Carey School of Business, Arizona State University, USA.

Serguei Netessine is Dhirubhai Ambani Professor of Innovation and Entrepreneurship at the Wharton School, USA.

How Management Academics Have Locked Themselves in an Iron Cage

GERRY JOHNSON AND KEN STARKEY

Our field of management as an academic pursuit faces threats that many acknowledge but our practices seem resistant to change. Scholars within the most prestigious universities, the research leaders in our field, are primarily concerned with research and publication, but there is limited impact of such published works, even within the academic community (judging by citation counts). This research has little impact upon the practice of management. Very few managers are aware of the hundreds of academic journals and their contents apart, perhaps, from *Harvard Business Review*. Students complain that academics are more interested in their research than they are of teaching yet it is income from students that pays salaries and funds research. The cost of publishing in the very top academic journals has been estimated to be between £200-300,000 per published article.

Nonetheless, the academic journal publishing route has become *de rigueur* for a successful academic career in a top tier school. Ironically for those who argue that business schools should aspire to be professional schools, the only audience for the research on which such publications is based is the very few scholars who review or read such publications. This has created a career path insulated from the subject of the field. We are faced with the threat of perceived irrelevance. Yet, despite more than 20 years of debate about how to alter this state of affairs, there is an inability or unwillingness of actors in the system to break out of it. This is not a new phenomenon or one peculiar to the UK. Don Hambrick's presidential address to the Academy of Management in 1993 was entitled 'What if the Academy actually mattered?'.

It is our contention that the business school system, at least in the UK and the US, has become an iron cage in which academics have allowed themselves, willingly or unwillingly, to be trapped. In using the phrase 'iron cage'

we have in mind Max Weber's famous phrase which he used to describe the end state brought about in the West by the processes of rationalization and bureaucratization. Our perception is that the iron cage of the publication imperative has become increasingly stronger over the last two decades. The unintended consequence of this is that management research has come to be seen as increasingly irrelevant to the concerns of practice. We need to recognise, understand and acknowledge the forces that have created this situation if it we want to make a case for the centrality of management research in understanding and facing the many challenges we face, in business and in society.

Here we set out what we see as the causes of the problem, framed, from an institutional perspective, as a system problem, and some proposals. It is, however, important to repeat that, in so doing, we do not argue here that the priority should be relevance and impact at the expense of good scholarship. This is not an either/or issue. We argue that **both** are needed. But the dysfunctional aspects of the publication system and its causes need resolution. It would be perverse of us, as management scholars whose careers have partly been built on publication in top journals, not to acknowledge the importance of research and publication. However, it would also be remiss not to express our concern about a system which we suggest has led to serious unintended consequences, not least because of the success of management education that has provided the financial cushion to maintain it. The most serious aspect of the current system is that it has become mostly self-serving and self-sustaining rather than responding adequately to the needs of external stakeholders - management, government and society.

DOI: 10.4324/9781003390633-6

Global Focus **Annual Research** Volume 1

How Management Academics Have Locked Themselves in an Iron Cage
Gerry Johnson and Ken Starkey
....

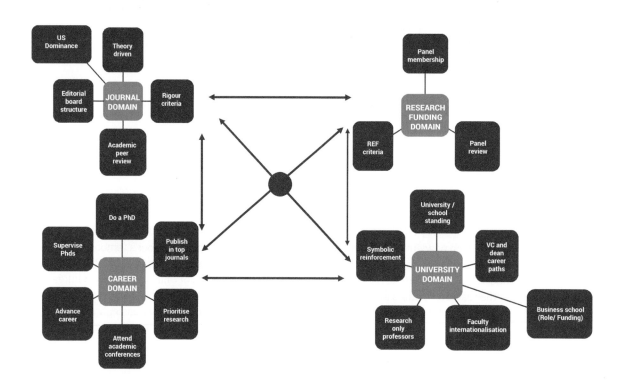

THE ACADEMIC ORGANISATIONAL FIELD

In the tradition of good scholarship we draw on a body of theory – institutional theory - one of the most influential, from an academic point of view, in management research, to make our case. We believe that such theory can provide practical insight and possible solutions. Institutional theorists refer to an organisational field as a community of organisations that interact more frequently with one another than with those outside the field and that have developed a shared meaning system. Such organisations often share a common technology, set of regulations and forms of education and training. As a result actors and organisations tend to cohere around a set of institutional assumptions, norms and routines held in common within an organisational field concerning the appropriate purposes and practices of field members. These are enacted in common strategies.

So what does this organisational field of management academia look like? We set out our 'model' of the field in the figure below.

This represents a system in which different activities and domains interlink to produce a whole that is largely self-contained. There are four domains – career, journal, research funding and university. In our figure we draw on our experience of the UK system and the drivers of the system we depict are strongest in UK and US schools. We would also suggest, however, that other countries are following this path, for example, in terms of the prioritisation of publication in top, largely US based journals. We suggest that this is the dominant direction of travel of aspiring top schools worldwide.

It is important to emphasise that these domains are self-reinforcing and mutually dependent upon each other. If we want to change the system then it is unlikely to be sufficient to advocate change in only one domain. The career paths of individuals start with doing a Ph.D., a key aspect of which is socializing graduate students into the importance of publication. Career progress is then dependent on publication in a limited number of journals that have publishing criteria established by senior academics, themselves a product of the same career path. In turn, the academic reputation and standing of the schools who hire these scholars are largely dependent on the same publishing output.

The field is regulated by shared norms, such as the journal rankings set out in influential lists (US A list; Financial Times, the Chartered Association of Business Schools AJG - Academic Journal Guide), which channel publication aspirations and are used, for example, by deans and appointment panels, to judge performance. The journal domain has become increasingly dependent on publication in top US journals. Career success is linked to this, although it is still only a very small minority of European authors who achieve entry to this elite club. These journals have a particular way of enforcing research norms which exclude other ways of framing research and scholarship. For example, it is very difficult to publish qualitative research or a single case study here.

Research funding is an important aspect of the management research field and various bodies have been developed to allocate this. In the UK, the main mechanism for allocating funding is the Research Excellent Framework (REF), a periodic review of research based upon peer review by a panel of experts recruited from business and management schools plus outside experts and advisers. A key aspect of this process is the review of publications, which again reinforces the importance of publication. Schools select publications for review based, in part, on the supposed quality of the journal in which papers appear. Papers tend to be considered more useful for this exercise than books. Indeed, very few junior faculty see writing a book as a sensible career option. REF performance is dissected by universities as a key reflection of a school's standing in the business school research hierarchy, as well as a source of research income. Top schools devote much time, attention and resource to optimizing research performance, including lighter teaching loads and even research only roles for star researchers, reinforcing the lessons that early career researchers draw from their experience of entry into the field.

HOW DOES THIS CAUSE A PROBLEM?

The first problem is the cost of the system. The cost of publishing has been indicated above. It may seem that upward of £200,000 per published paper is an exaggeration but consider the (often multiple) staff time taken by working on papers, the Revise and Resubmit process that can take years in the case of top journals, the review procedure and the fact that for every published paper there are 8/9 or more that are rejected. Yet, even among those published, very few of these will be read by managers themselves or indeed cited by other scholars. Publications that are actually read by managers, most notably *Harvard Business Review*, are deemed unworthy of serious consideration by scholars. (As an aside, when, a few years ago one of the authors discussed the role of business schools with the then UK Minister of Higher Education, the minister expressed surprise at the length of the AJG journal list, and declared, somewhat loudly, that there was only one he or his staff had heard of – *Harvard Business Review*!)

To maintain the publishing system business and its reputational effects, business schools must hire staff willing and able to deliver such publications who will argue that they need time and funding to do it; and such staff come at premium rates of remuneration. The role of research professor, liberated from the demands of teaching and administration, is seen by many as the pinnacle of an academic career.

The second problem is that, arguably, the field of management in 'research driven' universities does not deliver on the purpose of educating managers because it does not prioritise managerial engagement. Indeed the engagement with management is absent altogether in the organisational field we depict and, at the extreme, as in some US schools, it penalises such engagement because it gets in the way of research and publication. Schools that have sought to prioritise engagement with managers also run into a problem when staff, dedicated as they are to research and publishing, tend to be somewhat remote from the needs and expectations of managers. Some universities have created professorial career routes based upon teaching excellence but these remain peripheral. It is not then surprising if those outside the system see it as a costly, self-serving irrelevance.

The third problem is the inertial properties of the system. The different parties in an organisational field form a self-reinforcing network built on shared assumptions and behaviours that, quite likely, will lead to behavioural lock-in. Indeed professions, or trade associations, often attempt to formalise an organisational field where the membership is exclusive and the behaviour of members is regulated.

Global Focus **Annual Research** Volume 1

How Management Academics Have Locked Themselves in an Iron Cage
Gerry Johnson and Ken Starkey
....

Whether or not institutional norms are formalised, they can exert strong pressures for conformity not least because legitimacy within the field, be it at an organsational or individual level, becomes concerned with meeting the expectations within that organisational field in terms of its assumptions, behaviours and strategies. Moreover the career paths of young scholars are dependent on meeting such institutionalised expectations. These norms tend to become 'taken-for-granted'. Actors become 'institutionalised' such that they do not see the opportunities or threats from outside their organisational field and the norms they inherit are not questioned. Obviously, this creates a situation in which change is difficult, not least because institutionalisation makes the awareness of the need for change difficult to perceive. Business schools and their faculty seek to legitimise themselves through research excellence and either do not perceive any reason to change or, if they do, have little option but to conform to the institutional norms described above.

The fourth problem arises out of the search for legitimacy and the forces of mimesis that institutional theorists emphasise. Both individual scholars and schools have tended to aspire to achieve the 'academic excellence' displayed in the top schools in our field, an 'elite' dominated by top US schools. At one level, this is unsurprising since funding is dependent on such standing, as is the premium paid to attract those scholars able to demonstrate their ability to excel in the system. Historically it is perhaps not surprising that we have sought to emulate the U.S. system but one wonders if this is still the most appropriate model. One wonders if in the brave new world post-covid and after the financial crisis, we should continue to see the US Academy of Management, and the AoM annual conference, as the guardian of excellence in our field. Climate concerns are likely to undermine the justification for frequent air travel to academic conferences.

The fifth problem is that the system has re-inforced a divide within the business/management school world. There are those schools that are perceived to be 'research led' and there are those that are 'teaching led'. The former have little option but to conform to institutional norms: the latter may aspire to, or be encouraged to undertake research that allows entry into the system described above, but have little chance of doing so because the cost of entry is so high and their business model does not allow it.

WHAT MIGHT BE DONE?

Changing a highly institutionalised system is no easy matter but a number of routes can be considered.

Advocacy for change

Perhaps the first requirement is for the actors in the system to see it for what it is and understand why and how it is resistant to change. To do this there is a benefit if such recognition is advocated from within the system itself. We know not all of our colleagues accept the validity of our argument that we are faced with a problem that urgently needs solving. Indeed, we recognise that there is implacable resistance to our argument by some in the management research community. This resistance is often framed in terms of a defence of academic freedom. Part of our argument for change, however, is that we need to balance any claim to academic freedom with a sense of an obligation to academic responsibility in an applied field of study. This would seem to us to be a *sine qua non* if we accept the business schools are, in many ways, akin to professional schools like Law and Medicine.

Incremental change

There are already those within and external to the system who argue that it should be changed and are trying to make changes that they hope may gradually change the system. For example, some deans have sought to increase managerial engagement, involve practitioners more, for example, as visiting staff, 'executives in residence', 'professors of practice' and to change promotion criteria. It is, however, unlikely that changes within isolated schools will have much effect unless it is supported by changes within the publishing and funding domains. Promotion to a professorship through the teaching route, for example, seems to us a relatively isolated phenomenon. The irony here is that it is teaching the pays the vast majority of our salaries and funds much of our research time.

There have been calls for a practitioner-oriented management journal, but this has received little enthusiasm from researchers and little impress on the management world. Understandably, faculty do not see that publishing in such a journal would enhance their scholarly standing and would also require time and effort that could be better used publishing in journals that do. We wonder, nonetheless, if this might be worth pursuing for three reasons. First because its terms of reference and criteria of publication could complement those of current journals. A 'Journal of Applied Management Studies' could emphasise the examination, even testing, of management theory and models in practice- the equivalent of a clinical journal in medicine. Second, because it might provide opportunities for those who do engage more with managers, not least from schools that are 'teaching led,' to publish work that arises from such engagement.

The third reason leads to another possible course of action. Such a journal would be a change within the journal domain that might be mirrored and be part of simultaneous changes within other domains. If it were accompanied by changes to promotion criteria within the career domain, still further recognition of applied work in the funding domain, for example, this might provide impetus for change.

High impact system change

History is replete with examples when change was imposed on organisations from the outside when those inside refused to accept the need for change. Indeed, this is what research into the management of change teaches us. The idea of 'high impact system change' is that there may be levers for change that are particularly significant because they have pervasive influence. One historical example is the introduction of the the Research Assessment Exercise (RAE) in the UK in the late 1980s. This had the effect of radically changing the research priorities of universities because it changed their funding basis. It also served to open up UK universities to an international labour market because, in mimicking the academic criteria of the US system, it could also claim it promoted academic legitimacy in the UK. This, then, for good or bad, helped establish the system we now have.

It is argued by some that, in a similar way, the REF, or a reformed REF, could be an agent for major change now. There appear to be two problems with this. The first is mentioned above; the current impetus for change from the REF has not been pronounced. This may be because of the second problem; that radical change to 'relevance' or 'practice orientation' would not align with the institutionalised criteria of legitimacy in the field taken for granted internationally in what is now an open labour market. In short, we would lose many of our 'best' scholars whose main purpose in life is to publish in top journals. Ironically, for many of our colleagues, the desire to publish and to be seen to publish in top journals seems more important than the nature of the research itself. One effect of this is the 'salami-slicing' of research to maximise publication, ideally in 4* journals.

Another high impact change would, perhaps be if the criteria for publication in top journals themselves were to change; for example to demand much more significant evidence of practice relevance or impact. There has been slight evidence of this, usually, in our opinion, as an add-on rather than as an integral part of a publication. It is, however, difficult to see how major change in this regard might come about given that the editors and editorial boards of such journals are made up of scholars who are products of the current system.

Perhaps a more likely high impact change is that of external intervention, for example from government. Presumably government could determine that their own agencies for funding universities took a much stronger line in insisting on relevance an impact. More benign external intervention might be by business itself. If the business community were to take a serious interest, not only in the funding of research but in influencing the agenda for research, that might galvanise change. There are however many problems here. There is much less interest of business in the academic criteria most scholars would regard as important. The time scales that businesses work on are very different from researchers. Businesses see little need for or added-value in publishing in top ranked journals, although they do rate publication in *Harvard Business Review*. Substantial intervention in research agendas might be seen as undermining academic freedom. International comparisons are interesting here. For example, the French system of business schools is, much more closely linked with business than is that in the UK, so there may be lessons to be learned from that in terms of how to construct a different kind of institutional research field.

The most extreme high impact change would be a crisis. In the business school and university context, this might come in the form of major change in the demand for our services, possibly a major reduction in postgraduate international students, which obsoletes current business models, leading to financial crisis and major change. Undeniably unwelcome but a possibility. Students are becoming increasingly vocal in their demands for value for money and research time, unless it can be properly justified, might suffer as a result.

CONCLUSION

What might we do and what do we need to do to escape our iron cage? We need to agree a working consensus on the parameters of our current situation and its causes. In so doing we need to acknowledge the possible negative future consequences if we, but more important, the wider business school community do not engage in system change. We need to become less preoccupied with talking to each other

Global Focus **Annual Research** Volume 1

How Management Academics Have Locked Themselves in an Iron Cage
Gerry Johnson and Ken Starkey
....

and engage with other major stakeholders, actual and potential. If the cash cow bounty of large numbers of particularly postgraduate international students, with its large majority from China, paying very large fees, should decline – as it surely will at some point – then we will need to diversify our activity and our income streams.

We need to examine the system and Identify action points and strategies for change and endorse such strategies. If we as academics accept the need for change, then we need to decide how we as fellows can develop a wider awareness of the need for change. We might consider establishing small working groups to focus on different aspects of the levers for change identified and different domains. For example, as a group, we have contacts and might influence a wide range of stakeholders in the system – the academic, influential bodies in the field, colleagues, deans, journalists, politicians and so on. Here the role of Deans and their development is central as they consider the world we are moving towards.

We also need to reach out more to our European colleagues to discuss the system we are currently engaged in and by. Our final point is that this is a system with its roots in the US and its definition of what it takes to publish in top management journals. It might be that the time has come to redefine and recreate what it means to be a management academic. In discussing the seductive power of the iron cage, Weber also talked about calling and its values. Many of us feel that being a management academic is a calling. We think that that calling involves excellence in scholarship but it also calls out for a commitment to improving management and organisation through doing relevant and impactful research. We need to focus more on creating a new future vision of management responsive to the many challenges and crises business and society currently face.

About the Authors

Gerry Johnson is Emeritus Professor of Strategic Management at Lancaster University Management School, Professor of Strategic Management at Huddersfield University Business School and a Fellow of the British Academy of Management.

Ken Starkey is Professor of Management and Organisational Learning at Nottingham University Business School and a Fellow of the British Academy of Management.

Open up the Business School! From Rigour and Relevance to Purpose, Responsibility and Quality

ALAN IRWIN

MIXING OIL AND WATER

The *Financial Times* headline expresses it clearly enough: 'Academic focus limits business schools' contribution to society.'[1] We have heard this one before. As the argument goes, the push towards a particular model of high-quality research is getting in the way of practical application.

Despite the punchy headline, the *FT* article starts by heading in the opposite direction: 'On subjects from climate change to knife crime and racism in recruitment to kidney transplants, business school professors are conducting research geared towards making a positive impact on society.' It seems that at least some business school researchers are doing their best to serve society after all.

Are business schools obsessed with high-level academic publication and a narrow definition of research excellence? Or do they serve an important societal mission, working constructively with the business community and a range of stakeholders?

Based on my experience, both points of view are - at least partly - valid. Many of us working in the business school world can point to examples of the 'excellence' agenda pushing aside practical importance and societal impact. As one example, journal rankings and citation data seem to weigh more heavily within many academic hiring processes than engagement with practitioners or even teaching abilities.

Nevertheless, serious engagement with sustainability, societal inequality and business transformation can also be found - even if some of us would like to see more. For recent evidence, look no further than the 2021 report from the Chartered ABS Taskforce on *Business Schools and the Public Good*[2]. This presents a series of UK-based case-studies across research but also teaching, operations and engagement activities. There are legitimate concerns about the balance between 'academic focus' and 'contribution to society'. However, both undeniably exist within the contemporary business school.

So what's the problem? What is wrong with a situation where one group of business school researchers addresses practical matters while others seek to develop new theoretical models and contribute to academic knowledge? As it has been put to me, there are two kinds of researcher: those who seek truth and those who want to save the world. Can't we just agree that both are important – and then get on with it?

One answer can be found in a classic article from 1967[3]. Back then, the Nobel Prize winner Herbert Simon presented the business school as a problem in organisational design. The challenge for Simon was to balance 'the disciplines' and 'the professions': 'the social system of practitioners, on the one hand, and the social system of scientists in the relevant disciplines, on the other'. But as long as the practical professions and the academically-oriented disciplines peacefully co-exist then everything is fine. Right?

DOI: 10.4324/9781003390633-7

Global Focus **Annual Research** Volume 1

Open up the Business School! From Rigour and Relevance to Purpose, Responsibility and Quality
Alan Irwin
....

Wrong, said Simon. The problem is that if one leaves 'the disciplines' and 'the professions' to themselves then the goal of the business school gets lost. Access to practical problems leads to creative ideas, creative ideas help us see and act upon the world in new ways. And business school professors do not have the monopoly on creative ideas. Arguably, they have as much to learn from practical engagement as they have to give.

According to Simon's analysis, not every piece of research has to be immediately relevant. However, if there is no link whatsoever to relevance, then why be in the business school? To be even more provocative, without such a link why actually have the business school at all? Just like oil and water, the professional and the disciplinary will tend to separate. For Herbert Simon, the challenge for business school deans is to push against this: to mix the elements up vigorously and not let them settle into their separate silos.

This account of the oil and the water of the modern business school is a great help in understanding the tension between academic rigour and societal relevance which, as the *Financial Times* article confirms, still lingers over 50 years after Simon's original article[4]. Simon even provided some practical advice as to how to keep the mixing process going: don't, for example, allow the different groups to cluster their offices apart from each other. To put it bluntly, many business schools can boast on a web-site that they 'combine world-class excellence with real world impact'. However, if the people doing that work never actually speak to each other, and certainly never share ideas, what exactly is gained?

The implication is that we need to dig deeper into the nature of business school research and come up with some fresh ideas. It's not simply a matter of getting Prof. Rigour and Dr. Relevance to have a coffee together every few weeks (although that might be a start). It is also a question of how we define 'rigour' and 'relevance' in the first place. Couldn't we find ways of tackling these crucial matters without resorting to the old separation between academic excellence and practical application? Does this have to be a zero-sum game?

BEYOND THE GREAT DIVIDE

Several years ago, I was trying to promote a business school-wide initiative centred on what we called 'Business-in-Society (or BiS) platforms'. The idea was to draw upon research across several parts of the business school in order to address significant societal challenges.

Thinking back, the underlying case for 'BiS platforms' was very much in line with Simon's oil and water approach. And, since the business school in question was actually a 'business university' (Copenhagen Business School) my case at the time was that, rather than leaving researchers to sit in their own academic domains, we should get the full benefit of our substantial scale, broad research strengths and cross-disciplinarity.

One discussion with a senior professor (and, let me stress, valued colleague) really caught my attention. The focus of this exchange was climate change. For me this was an intellectually challenging and societally significant problem, requiring application of the highest-level scholarship to a matter of pressing concern – and one where management research is often relegated to a secondary position. Saving the world *and* doing world-class research? Who would not vote for that?

My colleague's reaction brought me down with a bump. Our debate focused specifically on research excellence. For the professor in question, excellence was basically judged by what could be published in top-tier academic journals. Cross-disciplinary and 'relevant' research might be interesting and worthy. It might score us some points with external stakeholders. However, it would never strengthen the publication record of an ambitious researcher in his field.

What for me was straightforwardly positive, for him posed a choice. Do we want to be a world-class research institution or a strong player in the regional business and political community? When an internationally-leading researcher poses a question in that way, it is not hard to guess what the answer will be.

The fundamental issue then is whether a concern with the societal impact of research detracts from excellence – not least by diverting precious resources. Or, as I was suggesting, does such a concern actually augment and stimulate research excellence – and at the same time fulfil an important responsibility?

Looking back, what is particularly striking is the rather limited, and decidedly binary, way in which our discussion was conducted. The whole problem with 'bridging' between high-quality research and practice is that it assumes two different sides: rigour *and* relevance, excellence *and* application, 'academic focus' *and* 'contribution to society'.

Global Focus **Annual Research** Volume 1

Open up the Business School! From Rigour and Relevance to Purpose, Responsibility and Quality
Alan Irwin

My professor colleague and I kicked the issues backwards and forwards. I don't actually think either of us changed our mind. I do know that the Business-in-Society initiative went ahead. But 'winning' the debate is not the only point. We need these open and challenging conversations if research strategies are to have any meaning. I came away more convinced than ever that the underlying model of rigour-relevance separation is no longer fit for purpose. In a world of cross-border, pan-institutional, co-created and trans-disciplinary challenges, is this really the best we can do?

Creative ideas are urgently needed. Let me offer just three. I do not claim that these are entirely new. They may not even be the most creative. However, I do think they can stimulate new perspectives and new conversations.

PURPOSE

John Brewer has proposed we adopt 'public value' as a focus for research and teaching across the social sciences[5]. Serious attention to public value suggests that we move beyond the language of 'academic focus', 'societal relevance', even 'impact', and instead address more fundamental goals and ambitions. What I like about this approach is that it quickly leads to the deeper issue of purpose.

What is it that business schools in general are trying to achieve? What is it that any particular business school is trying to achieve? How does a business school define its own role and its own ambition? Brewer puts particular emphasis on values such as trust, empathy, tolerance, compromise and a sense of belonging. Business schools might want to add other forms of 'public value' — public welfare, the creation of opportunities, sustainability, social equity, innovation. That could and should be a matter of serious reflection. It should also bring fresh perspective to questions of business school organisation, recruitment processes and incentive structures.

The 2021 report from the Chartered Association of Business Schools (CABS) on *Business Schools and the Public Good* advances this discussion in a number of important ways[2]. This is not surprising when one of the report's co-chairs, Martin Kitchener, has previously drawn on Brewer's ideas in order to develop Cardiff Business School towards the delivery of public value — or what he calls 'leading with purpose'[6]. The CABS report specifically identifies 'purpose-led' business schools, but also those where 'public good entrepreneurs' are active.

The point is not that we will all agree on the public value of the business school or take the same approach across different contexts and settings. The questions might be just as important as the answers. One good place to start is by asking for whom we are trying to add value and how.

In terms of business school research, purpose can be defined in many ways. It can also operate at a number of levels. The Business-in-Society platforms initiated at Copenhagen Business School were just one attempt to draw together researchers across different specialties in a sense of collective mission. Purpose cannot necessarily be imposed from above. However, attention to the purpose of business schools — including business school research — can be the start of a rewarding journey.

RESPONSIBILITY

There have long been discussions concerning the social, political and ethical implications of the natural sciences and engineering. What is the best relationship between science and democracy? What is the social responsibility of the scientist? How do we ensure a larger and more meaningful public engagement with new areas of innovation?[7]

Sometimes, these discussions arise in very general terms. More often, they relate to specific, perhaps controversial, areas of innovation and change: nanotechnology, driverless cars, genetically-modified food. Whilst these are often viewed as technical issues — as a matter for the experts — the point is that they simultaneously raise important societal questions. What about the ethics, the politics, the costs and the benefits, the overall direction of innovation?

Take the concept of Responsible Innovation: 'Responsible innovation means taking care of the future through collective stewardship of science and innovation in the present'[8]. The point is not that scientists should tackle these complex matters on their own. Instead, researchers are encouraged to play their part in facilitating a larger public conversation about the direction of socio-technical development — and the alternative futures that could lie ahead. Business schools should play a key role in these discussions.

Global Focus **Annual Research** Volume 1

Open up the Business School! From Rigour and Relevance to Purpose, Responsibility and Quality
Alan Irwin

Currently, important developments are taking place concerning responsible research in a business and management context. The Community for Responsible Research in Business and Management has presented seven principles in support of its Vision 2030: service to society; valuing both basic and applied contributions; valuing plurality and multidisciplinarity; sound methodology; stakeholder involvement; impact on stakeholders; broad dissemination[9]. Once again, a whole series of questions emerge: not least, about the practical meaning of responsibility. And once again, the discussion might be as important as the specific answers.

Just imagine a business school which plays a core role in society-wide reflections – and interventions - concerning responsible research and innovation: bringing in colleagues from the natural sciences but also multiple stakeholders in order to explore and help create new paths for socio-technical change. Isn't the business school the obvious place for such cross-disciplinary engagement? And wouldn't that put the business school at the very centre of intellectual, technical, social and economic development?

QUALITY

Let us re-claim the 'quality' word[10]. Quality is not only a matter of research excellence – although research quality is crucial. Quality is not only a matter of rankings, citations and evaluation practices. These are not ends but only means. Quality for me is about deciding what is important and setting our standards accordingly.

A serious focus on quality obliges business schools to consider how they define excellence in their activities. This might sound abstract. But it is actually down to earth and practical. What does a 'world class' stakeholder engagement look like? How do we judge excellence in targeting societal challenges and problems? What is the equivalent of the top-level journal article when it comes to cross-disciplinary engagement and helping tackle the challenges of sustainability or questions of social inclusion?

Quality cannot – and should not – be the same for all business schools. And even within the same school, there needs to be space for debate, reflection and difference. Rather than 'one size fits all', we might imagine business schools developing distinctive approaches: from quality in academic publications to quality in research-society relations, from quality in boosting opportunities for disadvantaged groups to quality in co-producing fresh approaches to old problems. The challenge is to re-make quality in new ways – and to keep doing so.

At least two attributes will be important in re-claiming quality. The first is creativity and the capacity of business schools to unleash the imaginative capacity of both their own staff and of a variety of stakeholders. That may not be as easy as it sounds. However, there is no shortage of potential in and around our organisations.

The second attribute is leadership. This is very much a matter of making choices: both about what to do and what not to do. It takes courage right now not to follow the international pack. And, perhaps understandably, there can be a significant strain of conservatism in our institutions. But isn't a sense of possibility the foundation for wise leadership?

OPEN UP THE BUSINESS SCHOOL!

Purpose. Responsibility. Quality. Each of these raises further questions: about their precise meaning in specific business school settings; about the relationship between business school researchers, other scientific disciplines and larger society; about how in practice they can be developed into business school-wide deliberations and conversations. As a former business school dean, I would never under-estimate these challenges. For that reason also, I would generally advocate an approach based on persistent experimentation, long-term thinking and institutional learning – in other words, mixing oil and water.

One leading critic has suggested shutting down the business school[11]. This article takes exactly the opposite approach. This is just the right time to take stock of what business schools are for. And instead of shutting them down, we should open them up to different ways of addressing purpose, responsibility and quality. We need multiple answers to the challenges faced and the opportunities from here.

Global Focus **Annual Research** Volume 1

Open up the Business School! From Rigour and Relevance to Purpose, Responsibility and Quality
Alan Irwin

....

We can briefly return to issues of climate change. For those who choose to engage, this is not about forcing all faculty to become activists or assuming that our only job in the business school is to find ways of putting the ideas of scientists and engineers into practice. Instead, it involves asking sharp questions about our purpose with regard to business and environmental transformation, identifying ways in which business schools can exercise (and encourage) responsibility, and considering how we can ambitiously raise the quality of our contribution. This is also about being unafraid to engage in areas of uncertainty, ignorance and disagreement. If we wait for these to be resolved, then it will already be too late to take meaningful action.

Purpose, responsibility and quality will not arrive neatly-packaged on the doorstep of the business school. Instead, interrogating, testing out and debating their meaning represents a serious, but also necessary, challenge. What all three concepts have in common is that they force us to ask larger questions and to recognise the possibilities ahead. Each of them also implies building sustained relationships. Business schools need networks and partners, critical friends and experts in different fields.

Rather than thinking about the business school in either/or terms, we need to open up to fresh ways of thinking about, contributing to and organising this crucial institution. We should open up the business school to purpose, responsibility and quality.

Footnotes

[1] Jack, A. February 24, 2020. 'Academic focus limits business schools' contribution to society.' *Financial Times*.

[2] Chartered Association of Business Schools (CABS). 2021. *Business schools and the public good*. CABS, London.

[3] Simon, H.A. 1967. 'The business school: a problem in organisational design.' *Journal of Management Studies*. 4: 1-16.

[4] Irwin, A. 2017. 'Mixing oil and water: on the co-production of professional and disciplinary goals in the modern business school.' In Huzzard, T., Benner, M. and Kärreman, D. (eds) *The Corporatization of the Business School: Minerva meets the Market*. Routledge, Abingdon and New York. pp.217-233.

[5] Brewer, J. D. 2013. *The public value of the social sciences: an interpretative essay*. Bloomsbury, London and New York.

[6] Kitchener, M. 2021. 'Leading with purpose: developing the first business school for public good.' In Lindgreen, A., Irwin, A., Poulfelt, F. and Thomsen, T.U. (eds) *How to Lead Academic Departments Successfully*. Edward Elgar, Cheltenham. pp.52-67.

[7] Jasanoff, S. 2016. *The Ethics of Invention: technology and the human future*. W.W.Norton, New York.

[8] Stilgoe, J., Owen, R. and Macnaghten, P. 2013. 'Developing a framework for responsible innovation.' *Research Policy*. Vol. 42(9): 1568-1580.

[9] Co-founders of RRBM (2017, revised 2020). 'A vision of responsible research in business and management: striving for useful and credible knowledge.' Position paper, accessible from www.rrbm.network

[10] Irwin, A. 2019. 'Re-making "quality" within the social sciences: the debate over rigour and relevance in the modern business school.' *The Sociological Review*. Vol. 67(1): 194-209.

[11] Parker, M. 2018. *Shut Down the Business School: what's wrong with management education*. Pluto Press, London.

About the Author

Alan Irwin is a Professor in the Department of Organisation at Copenhagen Business School.

Building Back Better:
Purpose-Driven Business Schools

MARTIN KITCHENER AND RACHEL ASHWORTH

Despite their many achievements, business schools are criticised for prioritising the achievement of outcomes, such as revenue and rankings, over the pursuit of their purpose.[1] Acknowledging the inherent variation among the world's many business schools, most were created with some idea of enhancing the public good by nurturing the management profession and conducting related scholarship. With many business schools having lost sight of their purpose, it is ironic that a reform movement is currently driving corporations to return to their purpose of generating "profitable solutions for the problems of people and planet, while not profiting from creating problems for either."[2]

As business schools display inertia while corporations change to pursue purpose, a rift is emerging between the interests of participants in the business school industry. On one side, employers want to hire the brightest minds to drive their purpose-driven companies, and graduates seek purposeful careers. On the other side, many business schools still operate teaching pedagogies, research agendas, and strategies that concentrate on the achievement of outcomes. This fissure exists despite programmatic calls for changes to business school operations issued by some journal editors, research funders, and former deans. It continues even though some business school academics play a leading role in the corporate reform movement. It carries on even though purpose is the first principle of the Responsible Management Education (PRME) initiative.[3]

To prevent the chasm widening, business school leaders must not default back into their pre-COVID approaches to achieving outcomes. Instead, they should build back better business schools that are purpose-driven (henceforth, P-Schools). This article illustrates the potential for such change from a report on the emergence of purpose-driven business schools in the UK,[4] and a study of strategic change at one of the first P-Schools.[5]

EARLY SIGHTINGS OF THE P-SCHOOL

A recent study of UK business schools examined ways that they seek to purposefully enhance public good through their four main activities: teaching, research, internal operations, and external engagement activities. Four broad approaches were identified. In the Traditional mode, strategic thinking is dominated by the achievement of outcomes such as revenue and rankings. As a result, purposeful activity remains a low priority and is restricted to a small number of discrete projects conducted by, what could be termed, 'purpose entrepreneurs'. In the Planned Development category, purpose-driven activity is reported to be a rising strategic priority, but it is still restricted to a small number of un-coordinated projects. A generous interpreter of this configuration might suggest a well-intentioned, and possibly temporary, disconnect between espoused and enacted strategy. A less kind observer might suggest 'purpose-washing'.

The Emergent category comprises schools which report that purpose-driven activity has risen-up the strategic agenda, and which can demonstrate aligned innovations across some, but not all, of the School's four main activity areas. In contrast, business schools in the Purpose-Driven (P-School) group share three characteristics, with each having:

(a) articulated their reason for being within a 'statement of purpose' that defines the positive contribution to public good that they will make,

(b) developed a purpose function to inspire and co-ordinate innovations across their four main activity areas, and

(c) started to develop approaches to reporting 'progress towards purpose'.

DOI: 10.4324/9781003390633-8

Global Focus **Annual Research** Volume 1

Building Back Better: Purpose-Driven Business Schools
Martin Kitchener and Rachel Ashworth
....

The P-School category comprises a diverse combination of seven business schools based at the universities of: Birmingham, Cardiff, Glasgow Caledonian, University of Arts London (UAL), Manchester, Queen Mary University of London (QMUL), and Queen's Belfast. This group includes five research-intensive schools located in major cities (Birmingham, Cardiff, Manchester, QMUL, Queen's Belfast), a school within a Scottish teaching-led university (Glasgow Caledonian), and one smaller business school specialising in the fashion industry (UAL). Despite this diversity, each P-School has begun to move away from outcomes-based strategies to state, coordinate, and report its purpose.

Stating Business School Purpose

All seven P-Schools display leadership approaches based on inculcating in colleagues a higher, clearer sense of their contribution to what the school does, and why and how they do it. In other words, a sense of purpose. A common foundation is that each P-School has articulated a 'statement of purpose' that defines their intended positive contribution to society.

The purpose statements of the seven P-Schools vary in two main respects. First, the local conceptualisation of purpose varies in each school. So, for example, while Manchester exists to promote 'Social Responsibility', Birmingham enhances 'Responsible Management', and Glasgow Caledonian enhances the 'Common Good'. The second point of variation among P-Schools is the source of the local conception of purpose. While four P-Schools developed the conception of purpose themselves (Birmingham, Cardiff, Queen's Belfast, and QMUL), in the other three cases, the local version of purpose was conceived by the parent university (Manchester, Glasgow Caledonian, and UAL). It will be interesting to observe whether the source of the local version of purpose has implications for staff buy-in, resource support, and sustainability.

Co-ordinating Delivery of Purpose

In addition to purpose statements, each of the P-Schools have established some form of purpose function to inspire and co-ordinate aligned innovations across their four main activity areas. This often involves the Dean, or some combination of senior leaders, performing a Chief Purpose Officer (CPO) role. The main objective is to inspire purposeful innovation from colleagues, and to report purposeful activity upwards internally, and to external audiences. At most of the P-Schools, the CPO role operates in collaboration with a committee or board charged with purposeful strategy development. At Birmingham this is called the Responsible Business Committee, at Cardiff it is the Shadow Management Board (described later), and at Manchester it is the Social Responsibility Committee.

Reporting on Purpose

To mitigate the risk of implementation gaps emerging between espoused strategies (e.g., purpose statements) and enacted activities, the corporate re-purposing movement recommends that organisations develop approaches to reporting on purpose. This involves extending beyond the standard reporting of outcomes, to include the production and usage of a broad range of capitals, including human, intellectual, natural, social, material, and financial. Among the P-Schools that have begun to address this challenge, the most common approach involves reporting to PRME principles[6], typically within Sharing of Information of Progress (SiP) reports, and internal processes of curriculum auditing and review.

Cardiff Business Schools' *Annual Public Value Report* is the first known attempt to measure and narrate a business school's progress towards its purpose using indicators of economic and social impact, sustainability, and staff attitudes. Whilst demonstrating the School's strong economic and social contribution and progressive model of governance, the report also found that the largest contributor to the School's carbon footprint is the travel of international students who are also, of course, its largest source of revenue. Whilst now evidenced, this tension has yet to be resolved. This is, in part, because resolution lies beyond the School, at the university-level of policy.

Despite the early stages of P-School development, and beyond the inevitable tensions that exist, their reported emergence in the UK indicates that some academic leaders have demonstrated the will and capacity to move away from the prevailing strategic pre-occupation with outcomes. Instead, they are trying to re-purpose their schools towards enhancing the public good. The next section provides a more detailed account of the process by which this is being attempted at one P-School.[7]

Global Focus **Annual Research** Volume 1

Building Back Better: Purpose-Driven Business Schools
Martin Kitchener and Rachel Ashworth
....

DEVELOPING A P-SCHOOL

Cardiff Business School (CARBS) is a large, multi-disciplinary academic community that is ranked 5th for research in the UK and is in the capital city of Wales. Since 2016, the School has pursued its stated purpose of enhancing public value by transforming activity across each of its four main activity areas. The change process began in 2013, in a standard way, with an in-coming Dean (Kitchener) conducting a strategic review of the School. In an unusual feature of the review, Kitchener conducted a search for a purpose-led strategic approach that suited the social scientific tradition of the School, and which offered an alternative to the outcomes-focused strategies that had come to dominate UK universities and their business schools. Unfortunately, Kitchener found little inspiration from either the practice or study of business school management. After a more than a year of searching, a senior colleague and friend (Rick Delbridge) suggested that Kitchener read John Brewer's sociological thesis on the *Public Value of Social Science*.[8] Reading that book led Kitchener to start conceiving the purpose of CARBS to be the delivery of public value.

The nascent idea of the 'public value business school', and Brewer's manifesto for change, were adapted to the School's distinctive character through a series of strategy development workshops that involved an extensive range of internal colleagues and external partners including: the School's advisory board, senior university leaders, employers, and government.[9] The aim of this widespread involvement in the strategy formulation process was to offer knowledgeable and committed colleagues the opportunity to contribute both to strategy conceptualisation, and to the development of aligned innovations across CARBS' activities. It was only after three years of this collaborative strategic process that Kitchener was able to formally launch the School's statement of purpose at a public event in 2018. Attendees were told that Cardiff, as the world's first public value business school, existed to:

"Promote economic and social improvement through interdisciplinary scholarship that addresses the grand challenges of our time, while operating a strong and progressive approach to our own governance".

In addition to this purpose statement, the second output of the collaborative strategic work was the following broad 'directions of purposeful travel' for the School's four main areas of activity:

(a) teaching and learning develops moral sentiments and capacities to promote economic and social improvement,

(b) interdisciplinary research addresses the grand challenges of our time,

(c) external engagement extends across a fuller range of partners, and

(d) a progressive approach to school governance.

Rather than following the more standard strategic approach of attempting to deliver key performance indicators defined by management, CARBS had committed to four broad directions of travel in pursuit of its purpose to enhance public value. In this sense, the strategy was oblique; no destination was specified.[10] Rather, it was left to colleagues to identify aligned innovations in each of the School's activity areas to advance the strategic journey. Progress in each area is summarised below.

Purposeful Teaching

CARBS colleagues have made clear progress in delivering public good through innovative teaching and learning that develops moral sensitivities and capacities to promote public good through economic and social improvement. The School's Education and Students strategy has produced curricula that are: research-informed, interdisciplinary, and Grand Challenge-oriented; collaborative in encouraging partnership with a wide range of stakeholders; and community-oriented, working in conjunction with social enterprises, small and medium-sized enterprises, multi-nationals and third sector bodies locally, nationally, and globally. Graduate attributes reflect public value with the aim of enabling students to be confident in their knowledge, skills and ability; ready to challenge societal and economic norms; empathetic and compassionate in dealing with others; aware of their reliance on one another and the environment; and healthy and happy.

Following Brewer, a key aim is to help students develop a better understanding of 'marginalised' workers who face challenges such as a lack of social protection, poor working practices, and wage stagnation. The School's Public Value Engagement Fellowships provide 'seedcorn' funding and workload reduction so that colleagues can develop relationships to underpin the co-creation of teaching. Examples include a partnership with Anti-Slavery International where students produced collaborative research to support Baroness Young's Modern Slavery (Transparency in Supply Chains) Bill and a collaboration with the Living Wage Foundation where module assessments involved working with employers on the Real Living Wage, with one student group credited in a local Health Board's recent decision to accredit to the Real Living Wage to over 2000 low paid employees.

Throughout their study, CARBS students are encouraged to consider how they can make a difference to the world around them. In terms of curricula development, public value is the central theme within a new MBA programme launched in 2021, and it is a key theme in the annual review of all programmes, encouraging multi-disciplinary and challenge-led content. On the new MBA programme, individual coaching helps participants identify purposeful careers, and the final, capstone, module links the themes of individual and organisational purpose.

By the end of 2018, there were signs that CARBS students valued the School's new purposeful approach to teaching as they contributed testimonials on the **School's "I stand for" initiative**:

I stand for_change

"It's not just about having a strong moral direction; it's having the inspiration and motivation to go out and do something. This is what I want the world to be. I feel I have the support from Cardiff Business School to go out and make a difference."

Ieuan Davies
Cardiff Business School student

I stand for_progress

"We have to understand the world we live in. Businesses, NGOs and government need to collaborate to impact the communities they operate in. It's about helping society progress together."

Shazerinna Zainal
Cardiff Business School student

Purposeful Research

Following the launch of the purpose-driven strategy in 2016, the School's Research Committee decided to re-direct its discretionary research budget to follow Brewer's manifesto and support interdisciplinary studies that address society's grand challenges. Following an innovative 'idea crowd-sourcing project' among faculty, the School adopted five grand challenges: decent work, fair and sustainable economies, future organisations, good governance and responsible innovation.[11] Of course, faculty are still encouraged to pursue their own research interests, and much public value research had been conducted in the School before this change process. The School's values have evolved into important Public Value principles that underpin our research activities. There is a focus on *co-creating knowledge* where researchers and stakeholders are equal partners in the research endeavour, *developing inter-disciplinary connections* through our multi-disciplinary research groups and new Social Science park, *sustaining a collegial research culture* where early career researcher engagement and altruistic academic leadership is promoted, and *inclusive engagement* involving a full range of social and economic stakeholders. The prioritization of public value criteria and ways of working in the allocation of research funding supports a growing portfolio of interdisciplinary research groups, public value research projects, and a stream of scholarship in public value. The public value research environment enables colleagues to contribute to their disciplines, and to society and in keeping with the School's traditions in critical management and open debate, some have also been inspired to write questioning the potential for purposeful change in the current political and economic climate.

PURPOSEFUL ENGAGEMENT.[12]

In addition to maintaining a business schools' conventional elite engagements (including its International Advisory Board, chaired by Adele Blakebrough MBE CEO of the Social Business Trust and co-location with the Institute of Directors in Wales), CARBS increasingly promotes economic and social improvement through a diverse range of collaborations. While some of these are international in scope, (e.g., UNPRME), others are local including the School's partnership with Llamau, a Welsh homeless charity. The School facilitates collaboration and engagement through monthly Breakfast Briefing sessions oriented around Grand Challenges and problem-oriented roundtables, while it has extended and strengthened relationships with a variety of SMEs, social enterprises and entrepreneurs, including under-represented and excluded groups such as women and BAME entrepreneurs. Partners such as the School's double cohort of public value entrepreneurs in residence are especially important to the purposeful change project because they help give credibility to an intrapreneurial approach that challenges dominant assumptions and practices, and they provide examples and learning opportunities to students.[13]

Global Focus **Annual Research** Volume 1

Building Back Better: Purpose-Driven Business Schools
Martin Kitchener and Rachel Ashworth
....

Purposeful School Governance

Under the previous governance approach at CARBS, and many other business schools, the combination of strong financial and academic performance, and compliance with legal requirements would constitute satisfactory outcomes. One of the distinctive elements of Cardiff's view of a purposeful business school is the commitment to delivering public good through a progressive approach to its own the governance.

The first steps began in 2013 with the collaborative strategy-making process and continued during its implementation. Almost immediately, this approach had the desired effect of inspiring many inclusivity initiatives including the development of an innovative Shadow Management Board (SMB). This body comprises a diverse mix of academic and professional service colleagues, most of whom have not previously held leadership roles. Established to widen participation and diversity in strategic decision-making, SMB includes faculty and professional service representatives of all grades and influences School decision-making by providing constructive challenge while developing its own policy proposals. The development of the new public value full-time MBA was prompted by a SMB review of the School's Postgraduate Education Portfolio. In 2017, the initial SMB chair became the first board member to join the senior management team, and she was then subsequently appointed Dean; the first woman to be Head of School.

Recent developments include the creation in 2020 of a Race Equality Committee designed to address continued societal and economic inequality, disadvantage and discrimination. Chaired by Professor Emmanuel Ogbonna, the Committee ensures that the School's workplace culture, learning environment, education curricula and teaching practices are diverse, inclusive and non-discriminatory, while addressing attainment gaps and amplifying BAME voices within the School.

The School's commitment to enhancing public good through its governance has also inspired a range of academic and professional service colleagues to work together to introduce a series of innovations in administrative areas including the production of the public value report, and a values-based approach to academic hiring.

CONCLUSION

This article began by arguing that as business school leaders emerge from the challenges of the COVID pandemic, they must not default back to their outcomes-based strategies. Instead, they should build back better business schools that are purpose-driven (P-Schools). To pursue this agenda, at least two linked changes are required. Among the business school community, leaders must combine their agency (albeit bounded) with a will to replace outcome-oriented strategies with purpose-driven alternatives. Fully recognising the complexity and magnitude of this challenge, this article has illustrated the potential for such change from a study that reports the emergence of P-Schools in the UK, and study of strategic change at one of the first P-Schools.

With different conceptions of purpose emerging in each P-School, all share three characteristics: they have articulated their reason for being within a statement of purpose; they have developed a purpose function to co-ordinate aligned innovations; and they have all started to develop approaches to reporting 'progress towards purpose'. The more in-depth account of development at Cardiff Business School illustrated a highly inclusive process that took nearly three years to produce a purpose statement and set of broad directions of purposeful travel in teaching, research, internal operations, and external engagement. Of course, the early purposeful innovations such as the Shadow Management Board are not yet enough to fully establish a purposeful business school. Instead, tensions continue to shadow the reform project, as they would within the many university contexts that are dominated by strategies to achieve outcomes.

At a wider level of change, the re-purposing of business schools will require a co-ordinated effort amongst diverse participants from the media, accreditation bodies, research funders, foundations, professional associations, students, and corporations. The corporate reform movement would seem to be a useful ally within any such coalition of the willing. It is also worth remembering that Milton Friedman, one of the inspirations for outcomes-focused corporate strategy, noted that solutions to crises often emerge from ideas that are lying around at the time. This article has argued that those charged with leading business schools should prioritise the pursuit of purpose over the achievement of outcomes. It is hoped that the emergence of P-Schools reported here may provide a source of inspiration for others who wish to build back better business schools.

Global Focus **Annual Research** Volume 1

Building Back Better: Purpose-Driven Business Schools
Martin Kitchener and Rachel Ashworth
....

Footnotes

[1] Kitchener, M, and R. Delbridge. (2020). "Lessons from Creating a Business School for Public Good: Obliquity, Waysetting and Wayfinding in Substantively Rational Change." *Academy of Management Teaching and Learning* 19/3: 307-322.

[2] British Academy. (2021). *Policy & Practice for Purposeful Business: The Final Report of the Future of the Corporation Programme*. London: The British Academy.

[3] unprme.org

[4] Chartered Association of Business Schools. (2021). *Business Schools and the Public Good*. London: Chartered ABS. https://charteredabs.org/wp-content/uploads/2021/06/Chartered-ABS-Business-Schools-and-the-Public-Good-Taskforce-Report.pdf

[5] Kitchener and Delbridge (2020) *ibid*.

[6] unprme.org

[7] A fuller, and more personal, account of strategy development at CARBS is provided in Kitchener, M. (2021). "Leading with Purpose: Developing the First Business School for Public Good." In A. Lindgreen, A. Irwin, F. Poulfelt, and T. U. Thomsen (Eds.) *How to Lead Academic Departments Successfully*, Edward Elgar.

[8] Brewer, J. D. (2013). *The Public Value of the Social Sciences*. London: Bloomsbury.

[9] Kitchener, M. (2019). "The Public Value of Social Science: From Manifesto to Organisational Strategy." In Lindgreen, A., Koenig-Lewis, N., Kitchener, M., Brewer, J. D., Moore, M. H. and Meynhardt, T. (Eds) *Public Value: Deepening, Enriching, and Broadening the Theory and Practice*, pp. 301-315. Abingdon: Routledge.

[10] Kitchener and Delbridge (2020) *ibid*

[11] https://www.cardiff.ac.uk/business-school/research/grand-challenges

[12] A more detailed analysis of purposeful engagement in P-Schools is provided in Kitchener, M., T. Levitt, and L. Thomas (2021). "Towards Purposeful Business Schools: Deepening and Broadening External Engagement". Available from author on request.

[13] https://www.cardiff.ac.uk/business-school/people/public-value-entrepreneurs-in-residence

About the Authors

Martin Kitchener is Professor of Management, and former Dean, at Cardiff Business School.
Rachel Ashworth is Dean and Professor of Public Services Management at Cardiff University Business School.

Gross National Wellbeing: The Future of Work

PROFESSOR SIR CARY COOPER

The last year and half of the pandemic has changed the nature of the workplace for many years to come. We have experienced a massive health crisis, enforced remote working, job losses, profound global changes (eg turmoil in the EU with British withdrawal, conflict between China and the West, soaring energy prices, concerns about future pandemics, etc.), and the beginnings of another major recession as governments withdraw support from businesses as the global vaccine programme begins to weaken the pandemic. The good news is that this has allowed us to reflect on the fundamentals of the workplace; about hybrid working, the role of the line manager, the length of the working work, how technology might transform the way we work, etc.

Flexible or hybrid working has been on the agenda of many organisations over the last decade (Norgate & Cooper, 2020; O'Meara & Cooper, 2022), but the pandemic has accelerated this process, and the future for many, except those who have to be at the 'coal face' of the office, will mean working substantially from home, returning to the central office when needed for team building, the development of new products and services, and to socialise with colleagues. This will have a profound effect on the role of the line manager, who will have to manage people, some of whom will be 'in the office' while others will be 'working from home'. We will need line managers who have well-developed social and interpersonal skills to manage a flexible workforce, individuals who can team-build in this hybrid model but also who can ensure that their direct reports have manageable workloads, realistic deadlines, are not overloaded and are coping with the intense pressures of the business recovery. Pre-Covid, the UK government's Health & Safety Executive reported that 57% of all long-term sickness absence was for stress, anxiety and depression. During the pandemic, the Office of National Statistics reported even higher levels of anxiety and depression (63%) in their large national wellbeing survey. These workplace

manifestations alone with have a profound effect on the role of the line manager going forward. Not only in line managers needing to manage hybrid teams of subordinates, to team build, provide a sense of purpose and communal goals but also in being able to recognise when their direct reports aren't coping or showing signs of stress when they are working substantially from home. Unfortunately, most businesses promote and recruit managers based on their technical skills not their people skills. So, until we promote and recruit people for managerial roles in the future, where there is parity between their technical and people skills, we will continue to see less effective team building, lower productivity and more stress-related ill health. As Mark Twain once wrote "If you always do what you always did, you'll always get what you always got". In the meantime, what do we do about the existing pool of line managers to enhance their social skills in the short-term. First, organisations ought to be doing audits of all their line managers, from shopfloor to top floor, on their empathic and emotional intelligence, providing training for those with low levels of social skills. In any case, HR usually knows where

DOI: 10.4324/9781003390633-9

the proverbial 'bodies lies', that is, which leaders are not as effective given their poor people-management skills. Second, HR needs to re-configure their assessment processes to find a way to ensure parity between an individual's social and technical skills when promoting or recruiting line managers. And finally, business schools need to go back to the 1970s and consider T-group and experiential training for all those doing management degrees and MBAs, instead of being exclusively 'cognitive input machines'! Managers ultimately need to manage human beings! Knowledge about HR, OB, accounting/ finance, marketing, economics, etc is part of the managerial learning process, but where in the curriculum does it get 'personal,' where individuals discover more about themselves and how they are seen by others in their interactions--so that they can manage a flexible workforce more effectively, are aware of when people are not coping, know how to psychologically motivate their teams, become better listeners, become more collaborative rather than command and control figureheads. At the moment, my own view is that business schools are doing only half their job, ignoring a vital aspect of people management, being a human being! Lao Tzu of Taoism wrote "a leader is best when people barely know he exists. When his work is done, his aim fulfilled, people will say 'we did it ourselves'".

We also need to consider what will happen when furloughing and government support for businesses (eg re-introduction of business rates, loses of direct government loans, etc.) will disappear, as we enter the post Covid era. It is predicted to lead to a major recession, leading to large scale job loss and intrinsic job insecurity for the 'job survivors', and it may be many years before recovery will lead to economic growth at pre-Covid levels. The health and

wellbeing of employees in all sectors will be at high risk of stress, and senior management will need to ensure that line managers, from the shopfloor to the top floor, get training to develop their emotional intelligence (EQ) and social skills to enable them to support their staff, and look after their own health (Bevan & Cooper, 2021).

The real challenge for senior management in the private and public sector will be to create wellbeing cultures, which retain and support their staff during these difficult times. If ever there was a need for health and wellbeing professionals, counsellors via employee assistance programmes (EAPs) and other support staff (eg. Mental health first aiders), it will be over the next few years. This is a great opportunity for HR, occupational health, workplace psychologists and other caring professionals to embrace these challenges and support employees and organisations who need help and solace. This is particularly important for small and medium sized businesses, the charity sector and various parts of the public sector, where HR and occupational health infrastructure is almost non-existent.

There is a growing movement toward a strategic approach to workplace wellbeing rather than an individualised approach such as 'mindfulness' at lunchtime, meditation, bean bags and massages at your desk! (Hesketh and Cooper, 2020). We are seeing more Directors of Health and Wellbeing, or in the US Chief Wellbeing Officers, reporting directly to HR Directors, and in some organisations directly to the CEO. Although wellbeing is not a regular Board agenda item on FTSE 250 companies yet, there are an increasing number of them highlighting wellbeing metrics in their annual or social responsibility reports, with Board

scrutiny from time to time (Cooper & Hesketh, 2022). Within the next five years, the need to retain millennials and top talent, to reduce stress-related ill health and to enhance productivity, senor executives will see strategic wellbeing at work as a bottom-line issue. We need to change, and the pandemic has enabled us to do this. The future requires that we change the nature of the workplace to meet the needs of employees and other stakeholders but change is not easy, as Machiavelli wrote in The Prince: "it should be borne in mind that there is nothing more difficult to arrange more doubtful of success, and more dangerous to carry through than initiating change....The innovator makes enemies of all those who prospered under the old order, and only lukewarm support is forthcoming from those who would prosper under the new". But now 'change is here to stay'!

When Winston Churchill was First Lord of the Admiralty in 1915, when things didn't go well for him in the Dardanelles campaign, and its fallout for him personally afterwards, he wrote: "Many remedies are suggested for the avoidance of worry and mental overstrain by persons who, over prolonged periods, have to bear exceptional responsibilities and discharge duties upon a very large scale. Some advise exercise, and others, repose. Some counsel travel, and others, retreat. Some praise solitude, and others, gaiety....but the element which is constant and common in all of them is Change.....a man can wear out a particular part of his mind by continually using it and tiring it, just in the same way as he can wear out the elbows of his coat...but tired parts of the mind can be rested and strengthened, not merely by rest, but by using other parts...It is only when new cells are called into activity, when new stars become the lords of the ascendant, that relief, refreshment are afforded." It is the great challenge of employers and managers to think about how we might change to support and help those who will be the walking wounded in our workplaces as we come out of the pandemic into a world recession. It is achievable, but we need to be innovative and challenge the orthodoxy of the past. Even John Ruskin, the British social reformer, reflected at the beginning of the Industrial Revolution in 1851 on the health of the worker of his time, that "in order that people may be happy in their work, these three things are needed: they must be fit for it, they must not do too much of it, and the must have a sense of success in it." This applies today in this ever complex world of work.

References

Bevan, S. and Cooper, C.L. (2021). *The Healthy Workforce*. Bingley: Emerald Publishing.

Cooper, C.L. and Hesketh, I. (Eds) (2022). *Managing Health and Wellbeing During a Crisis*. London: Kogan Page.

Hesketh, I. and Cooper, C.L. (2020). *Wellbeing at Work: How to Design, Implement and Evaluate an Effective Strategy*. London: Kogan Page.

Norgate, S. and Cooper, C.L. (Eds) (2020). *Flexible Work: Designing Our Healthier Future Lives*. London: Routledge Books.

O'Meara, S. and Cooper, C.L. (2022). *Remote Workplace Culture*. London: Kogan Page.

About the Author

Professor Sir Cary Cooper, CBE, is 50th Anniversary Professor of Organisational Psychology & Health at the ALLIANCE Manchester Business School & Chair of the National Forum for Health & Wellbeing at Work (comprised of 42 global employers).

Co-Creating Relevant Knowledge through Regional Virtual Collaboration: The Latin America Scholars Community Case

GABRIELA ALVARADO CABRERA

As business has become increasingly global in nature during the 21st century, business schools' international collaborations have gained more importance since schools look for greater relevance and bigger positive impact on society. In the case of Latin American business schools, the development of international partnerships and collaboration agreements has certainly gone hand in hand with the advent of countries' open economy and the ensuing rise of multinational companies, along with more regional firms becoming global. Yet, as the level of global trade is higher than the level of intra-regional trade in most Latin American countries, this has seemingly prompted an imbalance between global vs regional partnerships developed by schools in the continent[1]. However, this imbalance may change significantly in the future given the more recent challenges to principles of globalization arising from the global pandemic and the Ukraine invasion. Indeed, this may accelerate the need for stronger regional collaborations in handling such issues as supply chains and regional logistics as well as pedagogy and research in many areas of management education.

WHY TO PURSUE NEW INTERNATIONAL COLLABORATIONS AMONG LATIN AMERICAN BUSINESS SCHOOLS?

Just as in other regions of the world, while there are many reasons or goals for business schools in Latin America to look for international collaborations, some of the most common are:

- To provide their students and faculty with a global perspective by exposing them to different business practices and worldviews and better equip them to succeed within the international arena. This can be fulfilled through a wide array of collaborative agreements such as exchange programmes, study trips, visiting periods abroad, double or dual degrees, joint or consortium programmes, among many others. Still, one of the main issues for MNCs is to understand Latin America as a whole and become regional players.
- For complementary reasons. For instance, if a business school is regarded as the best school in Finance in the continent, but entrepreneurship is not precisely one of its strengths, to acquire meaningful insights on entrepreneurial topics and offer an enhanced learning experience to its students, the school might be interested in developing an international partnership with a business school that excels in entrepreneurship.
- To develop a unique position in a certain field (or region). In the previous example, the top-notch school in Finance could also be interested in partnering with a really good business school in Finance from another country or region, either for offering a unique programme in such field or for collaborative research purposes and build a very powerful international alliance. Furthermore, schools in Latin America have not really exploited the advantages of collaborating among themselves to develop content and

DOI: 10.4324/9781003390633-10

Global Focus **Annual Research** Volume 1

Co-Creating Relevant Knowledge through Regional Virtual Collaboration: The Latin America Scholars Community Case
Gabriela Alvarado Cabrera

programmes with a regional approach, neither to produce comparative research on the continent[2]. Collaboration and healthy competition should co-exist in the modern business school!

- To enhance the school's reputation. Sometimes, when looking for a collaborative agreement a business school in the region might be only interested in brand association for reputational purposes as partnering with an international strong brand can also enhance its school or programme brand value in the local market, greatly benefiting its graduates and faculty members.

- To enter and/or better understand new markets. If a school is interested in entering and/or better knowing certain market, it can think about partnering with a local school. Indeed, it is pretty common to see US business schools interested in entering an emerging market – like the Latin American market – through a joint programme with a local partner.

KEY SUCCESS FACTORS WHEN SETTING INTERNATIONAL COLLABORATIONS

Regardless of the purpose or reason behind why a business school is interested in developing a new international or regional collaboration, based on the experience that I have had when setting up either a double degree, a joint programme, or a research network, there are five elements that I have identified as key success factors when implementing such collaborations. These elements are:

1) First, to have a sound value proposition for both parties.
2) Second, to have a common challenge and/or strategic objective.
3) Third, to have certain degree of similarity between schools in terms of strategy, expectations, and structure. It is highly unlikely that a partnership between a small, private business school in Latin America and a large public university in the US can work. Decision making in the first one will be rather fast most of the times, while the large US school may need to wait for the State Board of Governors for approval. And no need to say that expectations in terms of number of students enrolled will be completely different.
4) Fourth, it is very important to have shared ownership and leadership, including a project leader in each institution and well-defined responsibilities for each partner.
5) And last but not least, collaboration depends on people, therefore true willingness to do it is an essential ingredient as well.

The presence of these five elements was essential in the creation and success of the Latin America Scholars Community, a virtual regional research network, as will be explained as follows.

THE LATAM SCHOLARS COMMUNITY

While the business environment in Latin America is characteristically Volatile, Uncertain, Complex, and Ambiguous (VUCA) and very different to the one that exists in developed economies – where most management theories were devised –, there is a clear predominance of US and European management content in schools of the region. There is a lack of knowledge on how to conduct business in the Latin American context and business schools have not seized the opportunity to create it, hence their contribution to the economic development of the region has not been fully exploited. Despite the greater weight given to research in many schools on the continent, this endeavor has not been focused on developing a deeper understanding of Latin America and business schools in the region now face the challenge of creating their own knowledge and identity[3].

Therefore, as part of the closing conversation of the first Latin America Business Education Jam held in partnership with the Questrom School of Business in Boston University – an event that attracted over 1,800 followers on Facebook from 17 Latin American countries including business schools' deans, faculty, students, and alumni in a series of discussion forums to share ideas with a common goal: to increase the value of Latin American management education –, two core reflections emerged: The pressing need to develop a distinctive value proposition for Latin American business schools and the potential impact of doing it in a collaborative way.

Global Focus **Annual Research** Volume 1

Co-Creating Relevant Knowledge through Regional Virtual Collaboration: The Latin America Scholars Community Case
Gabriela Alvarado Cabrera
....

There was a major criticism about adopting business school's models that were not conceived for the Latin American context. Hence, it was suggested that the unique value proposition for schools in the continent should emerge from studying and addressing the societal problems prevailing in the region. In this way, schools' common goal and challenge would be creating knowledge that is relevant to the continent and to the world, while increasing their impact on business and society.

Given the utmost importance of developing novel insights about the region and enhancing the value and relevance of Latin American management education, the idea of creating a research community attending the abovementioned value proposition emerged. As a result, the "Latin America Scholars Community", a network of researchers focused on developing content about the continent, was launched in June 2019. Its main objective is to promote collaborative work among professionals doing academic or applied research on five initial topics:

- Social entrepreneurship (current state, new business models, impact investing, social impact metrics, etc.), as well as all issues related to poverty, income inequality, and inclusive growth
- Corruption (economic and social costs) and ethical leadership.
- Family business (e.g., dynamics, evolution, professionalization, corporate governance, succession).
- Gender (e.g., female leadership, women in top management, levelling the playfield, support systems, among others).
- Management education (e.g., innovative teaching and learning methodologies, including hybrid and online offerings; stackable degree programmes; lifelong learning; micro-certificate programmes; academic vs applied research activities, etc.).

In addition, since there is a low level of overseas awareness of Latin American schools and hardly any appears among the top 100 business schools in the world, this initiative can also support schools in the region to address the challenge of developing a distinctive positioning in the global market and attract more foreign students, thus advancing the internationalization of Latin American business schools.

Currently, the network has a total of 174 researchers from 27 business schools located in Brazil, Chile, Colombia, Ecuador, Mexico, and Peru, and EFMD as global sponsor. To date, the number of researchers participating by topic is as follows: 68 in Social entrepreneurship, 37 in Corruption and ethical leadership, 32 in Family business, 29 in Gender, and 59 in Management education.

HOW DOES THIS INTERNATIONAL COLLABORATIVE RESEARCH NETWORK WORK?

Regular interaction among members of the network is virtual and by group of interest. In addition, a face-to-face event addressing topics from the different research groups is planned to take place every year. The idea is that the venue of the annual event rotates among business schools participating in the region and during the event attendees have the opportunity to share and discuss their research ideas and explore new collaboration opportunities, while expanding their research network and strengthening the existing one.

IPADE Business School was the host of the first event of the network "Building Research Communities among Latin American Scholars", where more than 80 participants from 16 different schools worked together to define priority issues to analyse in the region in the years to come. Furthermore, the event included a Deans' Panel about Value, Relevance, Impact, and Collaboration, in which the following topics were addressed: (a) key elements to develop a distinctive value proposition for business schools in the region, (b) effective mechanisms through which Latin American business schools can increase their impact on society and businesses, (c) how to include and foster the development of locally relevant content in the research agendas of business schools in Latin America, and (d) how regional collaboration among schools can contribute to the three themes previously raised. Due to the COVID-19 pandemic, face-to-face events are currently paused.

In March 2021, thanks to the support of EFMD Global, the Latin America Scholars Community website (https://latam.scholarscommunity.org/en/) was launched with the aim to continue promoting collaborative work among researchers of the network. The website has two main purposes: give visibility to the network, its members, and its research work,

Global Focus **Annual Research** Volume 1

Co-Creating Relevant Knowledge through Regional Virtual Collaboration: The Latin America Scholars Community Case
Gabriela Alvarado Cabrera
....

and providing a collaboration platform to facilitate interaction between researchers. In doing so, the website serves as an easy means to identify potential co-authors and get access to their contact information, previous work, and current research interests in detail. Yet, once the initial contact has been established, researchers may work independently of the platform. Some examples of collaborative projects that have arisen thanks to the Latin America Scholars Community include a research project on corruption and ethical leadership in Mexico and another one between Peruvian and Mexican business schools about gender.

On top of all that has been previously described, certainly, one of the most important contributions of the Latin America Scholars Community has been to create a wide and rich avenue that will change the culture of business schools in the region towards meaningful collaboration. As such, ownership and leadership of the initiative is shared through the sponsorship of all schools in the network, and it will have leaders by country as well. Besides, although it is not an international collaboration in terms of an academic programme, its results will undoubtedly enhance the value of management education in the region by providing students with relevant content that will help them to better understand how to conduct business in the Latin American context, thus giving them an edge in the global arena. It would be great if business schools from other regions could join this initiative and build a network akin to the Latin America Scholars Community in theirs, allowing all our schools to develop comparative research on common topics and contribute to continue advancing business education worldwide.

Gabriela Alvarado, DBA, is a Professor of Marketing at IPADE Business School where she also serves as Associate Director of Research and Academic Processes.

Footnotes

[1] G. Alvarado, H. Thomas, L. Thomas, and A. Wilson, *Latin America: Management Education's Growth and Future Pathways* (Bingley, UK: Emerald Publishing, 2018).

[2] Ibidem.

[3] Ibidem.

About the Author

Gabriela Alvarado, DBA, is a Professor of Marketing at IPADE Business School where she also serves as Associate Director of Research and Academic Processes.

The Competition Fetish in Business Schools: Challenges and Responses

RAJANI NAIDOO AND JÜRGEN ENDERS

Business Schools exist in a world with deepening social, economic, cultural and political fractures. These include an exponential growth in inequality, the return of absolute poverty and growing fault lines between those who have secure employment, those who work in precarious conditions, and those who are excluded. Migration caused by war and poverty has led to large scale suffering. Social solidarity within and across countries has been undermined, leading to rising xenophobia. In addition, urgent action is needed to protect the planet. Business Schools thus exist in a context that is divided by material and symbolic barriers where democracy is under threat.

Business schools, as institutions that are both nationally anchored and globally linked, with connections to business, government and civil society have the potential to play an important part in responding to these catastrophes and contributing to the greater good. However, while there are many opportunities, there are also obstacles. One such obstacle is the competition fetish (Naidoo, 2018). By this we mean that business schools appear to be trapped in a modern-day magical belief that competition will provide the solution to all problems. Competition is expected to enhance quality in research and teaching and lead to real world impact.

Different types of competition have been unleashed on universities with even greater competition in Business Schools (Krücken, 2021). These include quasi-market competition through which research and teaching is increasingly commodified for the purposes of income generation and government sponsored competition, generally termed 'excellence policies' where the core political aim is to identify world-class performance to provide positional advantage for global competition. In addition, status competition such as rankings through which business schools shape speculative value reign supreme. The various types of competition reinforce or displace one another or combine into new hybrid forms.

Competition is so powerful because it is fused with what Pierre Bourdieu has called doxa, which is an unquestionable orthodoxy that operates as if it were the objective truth (Bourdieu, 1988). Competition is deeply inscribed as common sense and as central to democracy. Competition is positioned as legitimate and just, resting on the assumption that all participants have an equal opportunity at the outset. Emotions reside in the heart of competition, producing an affective politics of naming, shaming and faming through which the fear of shame and the thrill of fame ignite strong competitive desires (Brogger 2016). In addition, forms of competition such as rankings rest on academic values that are upheld by the most powerful actors in the institutional field, with a clear interest in protecting the criteria that maintain these actors and institutions in positions of power (Enders, 2015).

DOI: 10.4324/9781003390633-11

Global Focus **Annual Research** Volume 1

The Competition Fetish in Business Schools: Challenges and Responses
Rajani Naidoo and Jürgen Enders
....

Clearly not all forms of competition are negative. There is substantial evidence that competition amongst researchers has led to major advances in research and that cognitive sense-making and sharing can build cognitive communities in research (Cattani et al, 2017). Meritocracy is fairer as a selection mechanism than criteria based on political affiliation or wealth. However, competition unthinkingly deployed everywhere can lead to negative consequences which act as barriers to business schools contributing to the greater good. In the next sections, we will outline some of the negative consequences of hyper-competition on research and education.

RESEARCH COMPETITION

The varieties of competition contributing to the fetishization of research has the potential to colonise epistemic frameworks. The strong link to reputational and financial rewards directs attention to what is deemed important and deflects attention away from what is not. In other words, competition is influential in defining the essence of research in business schools.

Scholarly competition based on peer review is a crucial mechanism to test and progress scholarship in the field of management studies and to build a common knowledge base for field advancement. However, other forms of competition interact in important ways with scholarly competition. Quasi-market competition which leads to close links between business schools and corporations can provide mutual benefit. However, there is the danger that a primary focus on the profit potential of research can push economic interest to override research undertaken for the public good. For example, the global financial and economic crisis has revealed the enmeshment of business schools with the ideologies of neo-classical economics and managerialism (Locke and Spender, 2011). Pressures for quick results from corporate sponsors may lead to tensions with the wider good; and patent agreements which prohibit dissemination to the research community can weaken the global knowledge commons.

Research excellence contests provide transparency in funding distribution, help business schools refine research strategy and develop mechanisms to enhance quality. However, there are also unintended effects. Scholars such as Kehm (2013) have shown how the German Excellence Initiative has resulted in more stratification, a downgrading of teaching and an additional administrative burden. There are also critiques that research excellence frameworks militate against 'blue skies' research, encourage dubious research tactics for maximizing citations (Alvesson et al,

2017). Rankings too are embedded in the business school ecosystem and work by abstracting institutions from their socio-political and economic contexts to construct a hierarchical ordering of institutions; with significant rewards and punishment (Wedlin, 2011). The high visibility of rankings construct a template of success, exerting pressures for compliance on different types of Business Schools across the world.

Excellence contests combine with rankings and a citation and publishing industry to construct standardised worldwide measures to access the quality of business school research. While this has the potential to create explicit, globally acknowledged measures of quality in management studies, there are also pitfalls. It has been persuasively demonstrated for example that the globally acknowledged 'top tier' list of journals is in reality mainly an American list cloaked as a global list drawing primarily on American data for an American audience. For example, the FT50 set of journal rankings is dominated by top US journals because of historical US influences and the dominance of the US paradigm in management education and research. Angus Laing (2022) has referred to perceived inbuilt biases of journal guides which rate which journals anchored in the positivistic American tradition more highly than those emanating from the more interpretivist European management research tradition. Adverse implications include the discounting on research in languages other than English, a devaluing of scholarly monographs and a disincentive to develop high impact, relevant research for non-American contexts. These narrow competitive mechanisms have the potential to reduce theoretical innovation in management studies as a result of closing down diversity. In terms of real world impact, research responding to the concerns of the powerful in rich countries is privileged while the crises facing the majority of the world's population living in low income countries receives less attention (Nkomo, 2017).

Given the increasingly inter-related crises facing the world, this is a situation in which the examination of the diversity of Business School models in developing and emerging markets is critical: country culture and context are critically important. This requires both competition and collaboration processes within regions for example in the different regions of Africa and Latin America (see Thomas et al., 2016, 2017 and Alvarado et al, 2017). This allows the sharing of curricula and research approaches that enhance the collective know-how of Deans in these regions.

Global Focus **Annual Research** Volume 1

The Competition Fetish in Business Schools: Challenges and Responses
Rajani Naidoo and Jürgen Enders
....

Hyper-Competition in Education

Business School education has come under increasing scrutiny as a result of recent corporate crises in the context of the global economic and climate crisis; and in recognition of the pivotal position and authority of students as future generations of managers.

The reconceptualisation of students as consumers of higher education in the context of hyper-competition; and the positioning of business schools as high income generating units has had both positive and negative impacts. Consumer mechanisms empower students through better information on course content, and greater transparency in relation to criteria and methods for assessment. More robust complaints and redress mechanisms afford students protection and the public availability of data from student satisfaction surveys empowers students to control elements of their learning. However there are also negative effects. Students who internalise a consumer identity may perceive themselves as passive and entitled consumers, abdicate their own responsibility for learning and confuse a momentary satisfaction of wants with educational outcomes (Naidoo et al, 2011). Consistent with this mentality is a resistance to expanding their horizons and engaging in education that is not directly assessed. Under these conditions, the student disposition generated has negative ramifications for the development of higher-order skills and, more importantly, for the dispositions and attitudes required for autonomous, lifelong learning.

In addition, business schools are under pressure to adhere to the criteria of major rankings such as the Financial Times, particularly in relation to the MBA programme. These rankings are based primarily on employability criteria such as career progression and salary increase. In this sense, commercial values become fundamentally important, compromising high level learning, responsibility for society etc. In this way, business schools ' abdicated [the] role of scientific, objective observers of business who are willing to engage in public discourse from the perspective of society as a whole' (Trank and Rynes, 2003, p. 199). An MBA becomes a value proposition primarily as a path to career security and financial riches.

This raises two main problems. First, while students are likely to demand education that links in a direct manner to employment, the rise of platform capitalism, artificial intelligence and technological developments make labour markets increasingly uncertain. Given current political trends, barely-regulated predatory capitalism combining with right-wing movements has the potential to deepen divisions amongst exploited and disadvantaged communities (for example between white and black working class young

people) through the manufacturing of fear, the inscription of hyper-competition and the spread of disinformation. We are thus likely to enter a highly volatile context with accelerating violence and an environmental emergency. In this context viewing Business School education primarily as a lever for employment reeks of irresponsibility.

At the same time, there is welcome evidence from contemporary surveys of students (for example the Aspen Institute) that there is a student led demand to embed people and planet issues in the curriculum. A broad, interdisciplinary, critical education which is not measured solely through market verification and student satisfaction may thus be viable in giving students the skills and the dispositions for lifelong learning and for enhanced careers as ethical, skilled and trustworthy managers. In addition, the incorporation of advanced leadership and management training to decarbonise the world and protect other sustainability goals is essential and may contribute to increases in high skilled labour demand.

Looking to the Future

How should Business Schools respond to these great challenges? How do Business School leaders face the formidable task of mediating between a complex internal environment with powerful professional autonomy and strong disciplinary allegiances while responding to competing external demands from governments, students, their own governing bodies, business and civil society? The hyper-competitive landscape often propels business schools towards certain type of behaviour to win certain types of competition while the nature of the challenges faced require collaborative leadership and dialogue to develop future responsive strategies. This requires an ongoing Dean-level sense making process to share ideas about approaches and futures. Business Schools need to resist the total onslaught of competition, to develop an understanding of where competition is useful and to identify the problems that competition cannot solve.

Global Focus **Annual Research** Volume 1

The Competition Fetish in Business Schools: Challenges and Responses
Rajani Naidoo and Jürgen Enders
....

In relation to research, rankings and excellence contests and 'A' lists of journals will remain a key signalling device for quality and reputation; and it is futile to expect that a single Business School acting independently can withdraw from these contests. One solution is for Business Schools to develop research strategies independently of narrow competitive frameworks and then adjust the positioning of the strategy to meet ranking and other goals. This could enable Business Schools to encompass critical research to create better understanding and support for-profit and public and civil sector organisations, while presenting critical analyses of the effects of such organisations on the public good. There are now alternative visions which can be drawn upon for research strategies in which economic development is seen as important but in the service of other goals such as security, more secure livelihoods, and political and cultural freedoms (Gough and Wood, 2006). Business Schools need to engage in resisting pressures for corporate claims to trump, and ensure that profitability is set alongside other values, such as social justice and ecological well-being. A good example of such a research strategy is our own University of Bath School of Management's Research4Good focus which aims to improve lives, enhance communities and strengthen the economy through research programmes on modern slavery, sustainability and the value of accessible and quality education in low-income countries. Responsible Research for Business and Management (RRBM) is a further example of scholarly communities coming together to inspire and supporting credible and useful research in the business and management disciplines which has a positive impact on organisations, communities and countries.

The A list of journals can also be supplemented by business school alliances coming together to develop criteria to select regionally relevant high-quality journals which can be officially recognised alongside the American top tier journals for tenure and promotion in specific regions. This can be supplemented by collective, concerted and sustained action to promote regional and scholarly diversity in the lists which are currently hegemonic and which act as an isomorphic pressure.

Business Schools can also move beyond the 'student-as-disciple' or student-as passive-consumer' model to recognising students as co-producers. From this perspective, students will be configured as uniquely skilled participants, who, for the production of value-in-use to occur, must be given the opportunity to share their knowledge and make significant inputs to the learning and teaching process. This also requires a new understanding of the role of faculty. Co-creation when applied to pedagogical relations represents a more dialogical model that no longer privileges the Faculty's vision of education but provides resources which foster the creation of specific innovative forms of student participation as a contributor to quality, satisfaction and value. In this way the problems encountered by a model based on the notion of a passive and instrumental student consumer are replaced by the notion of an engaged and co-creative learner which also leads to action based and experiential learning.

Thought must be given to how to balance the intrinsic and extrinsic interests of students and how to develop a more holistic and critical model of management education so that Business Schools contribute to developing global citizens with critical reasoning while enhancing students' abilities to respond to some of the most serious threats that democracy faces. Alternative conceptions of Business School education have emerged including responsible management education and education for sustainability. However, these courses are often optional, stand-alone courses and are often not integrated fully into the curriculum. An important programme is the University of Bath Doctor of Business Administration in Higher Education Management which has a global component as well as a Future Leaders Programme tailored for South African higher education managers. Attracting higher education leaders from more than 60 countries, the curriculum is explicitly interdisciplinary, combines research with advanced leadership skills and is global beyond Anglo-Saxon perspectives. The programme enhances criticality, reflexivity and ethical awareness in higher education leaders including Business School Deans. A further holistic example is the liberal arts curriculum developed for undergraduate education at the Singapore Management School (Thomas et

Global Focus **Annual Research** Volume 1

The Competition Fetish in Business Schools: Challenges and Responses
Rajani Naidoo and Jürgen Enders
....

al, 2023). Experimenting with such models across various national contexts is vitally important for a more just and ecologically more sustainable world enhanced by student centred learning.

Apart from the important reasons outlined above, there is another important reason for Business Schools to deviate from some of the specific tracks of the competition fetish which led to increasing isomorphism within institutional tiers. Increasing competition will arise not simply from other Business Schools but from a booming list of private education, technology and consulting firms and mega-platform based global corporations all providing education that promise career and salary advancement. In order to survive and develop resilience, Business Schools need to differentiate themselves from such providers and one of the ways in which this can be done is to focus on marrying employability with wider education goals which include sustainability, global citizenship and inclusive leadership; and develop research which is critical, novel, trustworthy and interdisciplinary and creates scholarly, policy and leadership impact.

References

Alvarado, G., Thomas, H., Thomas, L and Wilson, A. (2018) *Latin America: Management Education Growth and Future Pathways*. Bingley UK: Emerald Publishing

Alvesson, M., Yiannis, G., & Paulsen, R. (2017). *Return to Meaning: A Social Science with Something to Say*. Oxford University Press.

Brøgger K (2016) The rule of mimetic desire in higher education: governing through naming, shaming and faming. *British Journal of Sociology of Education 37*(1):72-91.

Bourdieu P (1988) *Homo Academicus*. Cambridge: Polity Press.

Cattani, G., Porac, J. and Thomas, H. (2017) Categories and Competition. *Strategic Management Journal.* 28: 64-92

Enders, J. (2015) The academic arms race: international rankings and global competition for world-class universities. In: Pettigrew AW, Cornuel E and Hommel U (eds) *The Institutional Development of Business Schools*. Oxford: Oxford University Press:155-175

Gough, I. and Wood, G. (2006) A comparative welfare regime approach to global social policy. *World Development, 34* (10):1696-712

Kehm, B.M. (2013) To be or not to be? The Impacts of the excellence Initiative on the German system of higher education. In Shin JC, Kehm, BM (eds) *Institutionalization of World-Class University in Global Competition*. Dordrecht: Springer, pp 81-97

Krücken, G. (2021) Multiple competitions in higher education: a conceptual approach, *Innovation, 23*(2) 163-181, DOI: 10.1080/14479338.2019.1684652eferences

Laing, A (2022) Whether (or wither) academic journal guides? *Global Focus* Volume 2; 25 May 2022 https://www.globalfocusmagazine.com/whether-or-wither-academic-journal-guides/

Locke, R.R. and Spender, J-C (2011) *Confronting Managerialism: How the Business Elite and Their Schools Threw Our Lives Out of Balance*. Zed Books

Naidoo, R. (2018). The competition fetish in higher education: Shamans, mind snares and consequences. *European Educational Research Journal, 17*(5), 605-620. https://doi.org/10.1177/1474904118784839

Naidoo R, Shankar A and Veer E (2011) The consumerist turn in higher education: Policy aspirations and outcomes. *Journal of Marketing Management 27*(11-12):1142-62.

Nkomo, S.M. (2009) The Seductive Power of Academic Journal Rankings: Challenges of Searching for the Otherwise. *Academy of Management and Learning Vol 8* (1):106-112

Thomas, H., Lee, M., Thomas, L and Wilson, A. (2016, 2017) *Africa: The Management Education Challenge: Volumes 1 and 2*. Bingley, UK: Emerald Publishing

Thomas, H., Wilson, A and Lee, M. (2023 forthcoming) *Creating a New Management University: Tracking the Strategy of Singapore Management University in Singapore (1997-2020)*. Abingdon, UK: Routledge

Trank, C.Q. and Rynes, S.L. (2003) Who Moved our Cheese? Reclaiming Professionalism in Business Education. *Academy of Management and Learning Vol 2* (2):189-205

Wedlin L (2011) Going global: Rankings as rhetorical devices to construct an international field of management education. *Management Learning 42*(2):199-218

About the Authors

Professor Rajani Naidoo is Vice-President (Community and Inclusion), UNESCO Chair and Co-Director of the International centre for Higher Education at the University of Bath, UK.

Jürgen Enders is Professor and Co-director of the International Centre for Higher Education Management in the School of Management at the University of Bath. He is a Fellow of the Academia Europaea, the German Academy of Science and Engineering, and the Society for Research into Higher Education.

Contextualising Change with Social Network Analysis

KENNETH QUA AND BARBARA SPORN

Unlike typical organisations where the essential knowledge and resources for change flow through formalised hierarchies, structures and trainings, universities often have diverse and disjointed schools and faculties that all coexist under a singular brand. How can universities pursue change management projects effectively given their unique organisational characteristics and the complexity of their internal structure? Social network analysis (SNA) has shed light on underlying forces that affect consensus building, community decision making, belief systems and the diffusion and adoption of innovations[1].

What makes SNA distinctive from other theoretical approaches? First and foremost, the focus on the relationships as the units of analysis and the structure of those relationships is a departure from the attribute-based analysis prevalent in economics and other social sciences. SNA is useful in allowing us to augment and contextualise attribute-based data with the relationships between actors having an effect on the actors themselves. Secondly, SNA's focus on social influences also make it distinct from theories in decision-making research such as utility theory and prospect theory that consider individuals who make decisions impervious to external influences. For group decision-making and consensus building, the network approach of analysing how members of the group influence each other is crucial to understanding the process of consensus building[1]. It should be noted that this does not imply that SNA disregards the autonomy of individual agency nor does it suggest that individuals are merely subjects to the whims of the group. The point of SNA is to draw insights from the relationships between actors to deepen the understanding of why individuals, groups or organisations make the decisions that they do.

For change in higher education, social networks facilitate knowledge transfer, increase learning and provide social capital which mitigates the risks associated to change[2]. While faculty resistance or poor governance may be possible sources of failure for change management, SNA can serve as both a diagnostic and tactical tool to understand and execute change management strategies effectively. Understanding how informal ties within an organisation can not only provide contextual clues on how to best communicate a strategy but also direct action towards key actors within a network. The authors conducted a study that used SNA to compare two business universities that embarked on a similar change project, i.e., introducing an interdisciplinary bachelor's programme.

DOI: 10.4324/9781003390633-12

Global Focus **Annual Research** Volume 1

Contextualising Change with Social Network Analysis
Kenneth Qua and Barbara Sporn
....

INTRODUCING INTERDISCIPLINARY PROGRAMMES: A CASE STUDY COMPARISON

For our study, a business university in Singapore and a business university in Austria were selected. Both universities recently introduced successful interdisciplinary programmes, which are often viewed as challenging change projects due to the nature of involving stakeholders from various disciplines. Semi-structured interviews were conducted between February to May 2020 with key committee members from each university either in-person or virtually. For the sake of confidentiality, the names of the universities that were chosen for this study were changed and the names of the interviewees redacted. Table 1 describes the profiles for each interviewee.

Lion University

Lion University (LU) is a prestigious business university in Singapore which consists of six different schools specializing in disciplines ranging across business, social sciences and law. Founded at the turn of the millennium, the university is just over two decades old and offers various programmes in each of their respective six schools along with come interdisciplinary programmes which span across several schools. LU has a modest student population of around 10,000 students with over 250 faculty. LU launched their interdisciplinary programme in early 2016 that was offered under the School of Social Sciences (SOSS). The interdisciplinary nature of the major integrates courses from two other faculties in LU, namely, the School of Economics (SOE) and the School of Law (SOL).

Stag University

Stag University (SU) is a business university in Austria that is renowned in Europe for its thought leadership, state-of-the-art campus and robust academic credentials. The university was founded towards the end of the nineteenth century making it significantly older and more mature compared to SU. It has served as a pivotal institution for the education of business and economics in Austrian society. Unlike LU, the university leadership in SU has an element of shared governance and decentralization, notably with their Senate which consists of professors, junior professors and students. SU also boasts a much bigger student population with over 25,000 students and over twice number of faculty compared to LU. SU introduced their interdisciplinary programme in the 2018 winter semester. The programme's content adopts an interdisciplinary approach spanning across various departments like Economics, Marketing, Accounting and Law amongst others. While SU and LU might differ in age and size, both universities share a common belief in management education with a liberal arts tradition.

Interviewee	University	Position	School/ Department
1	Lion University	Associate Dean	Social Sciences
2	Lion University	Associate Dean	Economics
3	Stag University	Department Head	Business
4	Stag University	Vice-Provost	Academic Programmes and Student Affairs

RESULTS

LU had a robust system of hierarchy which led to the speedy deliberation and implementation process of their programme. On the other hand, the instrument of shared governance in SU led to an iterative process of refinement that sought to integrate the goals and expectations of various stakeholders as consensus and agreement was built. Institutional governance was the key contextual difference that influenced most of the SNA themes which we cover in more detail. A summary of the results can be seen in Table 2.

SNA Themes	Lion University	Stag University
Strength of Ties	Strong ties were important between actors inside committee	Strong ties were important between actors from committee and actors around the network
Central Actors	Not significant	Important in negotiation process to win support of central actors
Diversity of Ties	Both universities had formal bodies that encouraged bridging ties	
Nature of Interaction	Dependent on the governance style of university	
Subgroups	Both universities emphasised small teams	

Strength of Ties

Strong ties would be characterised as two parties who share 'frequent interaction, extended history, and intimacy or mutual confiding between parties'[2]. Strong ties reduce the likelihood of resistance and increase the opportunity to understand the complexities of all the stakeholders that are involved in the change implementation[3]. The most fundamental similarity between both case studies is the clear presence of strong ties being a factor for the successful planning and implementation of the interdisciplinary programmes. The difference, however, lies in where these strong ties are found.

For LU, the strong ties were within their committee. This allowed for a quick curriculum building process where each member worked independently within the given curriculum structure after a single meeting. Due to the system of shared governance in SU, strong ties were instrumental in connecting committee members with people around the organisation who were not directly involved in the planning. These strong ties aided in the negotiation process for the interdisciplinary programme's approval in the Senate.

The strong ties that were crucial in the change initiative for LU and SU differed as a function of their institutional governance. With the top-down hierarchy of LU, the strong ties were important in the planning stages as core members of the committee were decision makers and once consensus was built at the top, implementation was rolled out expeditiously through the organisation. In contrast, the importance of strong ties for SU weighed heavily on the committee members being connected to the professors in the Senate.

Central Actors

Centrality is a fundamental concept in SNA and central actors are the ones who 'occupy central position in the network' and 'tend to be more visible, they tend to know many people and many people know them'[4](p96). Central actors are individuals with the most number of ties to other actors in an organisation leading these individuals to have 'more access to information and knowledge, have a better ability to communicate throughout the system, and are likely to have great influence within the network'[2]. In the case study of LU, the centralised university governance left little need to question the functional power of central actors given the executive authority of senior leadership. However, with the lobbying process involved in winning support amongst SU's formal bodies like the Association of Professors and the Senate, central actors played an influential role in the change process for the programme's implementation. Gaining the support of opinion leaders in SU assisted the committee in building agreement and approval among various parts of the organisation.

In short, central actors and, within the same vein, opinion leaders, were important in the negotiation process for SU due to their shared governance structure. The shared governance structure translated the influence of opinion leaders and central actors into informal power in the formal bodies that had voting rights. With voting power being dispersed across the formal bodies, central actors would have a superordinate position to influence change due to their highly connected position. This is opposed to a centralised governance structure where it would be more crucial to be connected with the actors that possess authority.

Diversity of Ties

Diversity of ties is also referred to as heterophily which describe ties that 'span multiple knowledge sources or cut across structural holes'[2]. As expected for a change initiative that is about interdisciplinarity, there were diverse ties in both committees for LU and SU. The committee members for LU were associate deans from each participating faculties, while similarly in SU there was a representative professor from the business department and the economics department for their interdisciplinary programme. In both universities, formal bodies within the organisation facilitated tie formation across the typically siloed departments in higher education. LU had a University Curriculum Committee which consists of members from different faculties meeting regularly, thus allowing for the awareness of diverse sets of interests and constraints from each school to be shared. The Senate and various other formal organisations in SU served a similar function as fora that brought together diverse sets of individuals. These structures, while artificial, in LU and SU helped to reduce the heterophily that is characteristic to higher education institutions.

Nature of Interaction

Nature of interaction can be characterised as being one-way, where information flows only from one source or two-way, where information sharing is mutual. In theory, two-way interaction allows for greater learning and schema change which is ideal for successful change implementation[2]. The case study of LU showed otherwise with the planning and implementation of the interdisciplinary programme stemming from mostly one-way interactions across different levels of the organisation. Conversely, in SU two-way interaction was the rule regarding the nature of interaction. It was imperative for SU's project members to engage in a two-way dialogue with other faculty to understand and express their goals and concerns. The intensive negotiation process by the project members in SU embody these principles where individual meetings with different department heads allowed the programme's curriculum to evolve and eventually succeed in the Senate vote.

The difference in institutional governance again played a major role as the element of shared governance necessitated the need for a two-way interaction for SU's introduction of their interdisciplinary programme. The efficient hierarchy at LU made the success of their programme's introduction less contingent on the nature of interaction where a one-way interaction sufficed.

Subgroups

All four interviewees mentioned that they were deliberate in keeping the group size for the committees small. In SNA, these smaller networks that exist within a whole network but are bigger than triads are known as subgroups[4]. Cohesive subgroups have been observed to be important for change projects as they '[enable] information flow, [change] attitudes and [create] resources necessary for change'[2]. Having an effective subgroup with the right expertise allowed the committee at LU to build consensus quickly and collaborate without any major disagreements. Subgroups not only allow greater trust to be fostered amongst the actors but also constrain the number of interests involved which moderates the possibilities for conflict. SU's Department Head for Business only agreed to work on the project if there was a maximum of 3 people on the committee and was insistent that he "wouldn't do it if there was too many people because you cannot make it work". More importantly, the main committee for SU was a subgroup of brokers who had strong bridging ties with the rest of the greater network. Brokers are actors that connect structural holes which exist among disconnected subgroups[4]. In order to influence and negotiate with the larger network of SU, the committee members sought to individually meet with departments that they were more

connected to. In essence, it was through SU's committee subgroup where change attitudes could flow smoothly through the network that may originally have parts that were disconnected.

CHANGE WITHIN CONTEXT

Underpinning the differences between LU and SU is their institutional governance. LU's top-down hierarchy is expressed not only in their formal organisations like the University Curriculum Committee but also in the way change is implemented in the university. Change initiatives flow down from a decision made by senior management through various levels of leadership. Subgroups that connect the different faculties also lie in a hierarchy. When SNA is applied to understanding LU's planning and implementation process a cohesive subgroup with heterophilous ties at the centre of the change initiative can be observed. Having the right people in the subgroup enabled LU's expeditious planning and implementation of their interdisciplinary programme.

The bottom-up culture in SU is also prominently expressed through the structure of the social network and how actors within the network interact. With formal organisations like the Senate comprising of not only professors, but students and junior professors, we can observe a deliberate effort from the organisation to provide a point of connection between diverse organisational subunits at different levels. Given the voting power of each professor in SU, change actors pushing for initiatives are, by design, compelled to engage in two-way interactions with the network. The intensity and frequency of negotiations involved led to a more time-intensive process which likely built greater consensus throughout the organisation. While SU has a different process compared to LU, the core of the change initiative was also subgroup with the right people. For SU, the right people consisted of influential opinion leaders whom could convince and learn from the greater network to adapt the interdisciplinary programme for its eventual successful form.

Global Focus **Annual Research** Volume 1

Contextualising Change with Social Network Analysis
Kenneth Qua and Barbara Sporn
....

CONCLUSION

In summary, our study investigated the challenges of implementing widespread systematic changes given the mounting external pressure for universities to evolve. SNA was used as a lens to understand how universities are organised with a focus on informal networks. Five SNA themes were highlighted which give a greater understanding of how a change strategy might potentially unfold, allowing for rectifications in the strategy itself or the implementation approach in order to maximise the effectiveness.

As observed in the case study comparison, change management strategies work best when tailored to the organisational context. In institutions of centralised hierarchies, strong ties across departments at each level are optimal for change to spread throughout the network. In decentralised systems where power is dispersed throughout the network, identifying brokers, opinion leaders and central actors are crucial to the change process. Fostering the right ties is crucial and organisations should analyse whether their committees are facilitating the creation of these strong bridging ties. Ensuring a diversity of ties with individuals from varying parts of the organisation meeting up regularly can be the first step to creating such bridging ties.

In summary, SNA can be an invaluable tool for leadership in people-oriented and knowledge-intensive industries that need a pulse on the informal structures within their organisations. Having this pulse will allow even the most complex of organisations to nimbly and effectively navigate and evolve through uncertainty.

Footnotes

[1] Wasserman S, Faust K. *Social Network Analysis*. Vol 8. Cambridge University Press; 1994. doi:10.1017/CBO9780511815478

[2] Kezar A. Higher Education Change and Social Networks: A Review of Research. *J Higher Educ*. 2014;85(1):91-125. doi:10.1353/jhe.2014.0003

[3] Tenkasi R V., Chesmore MC. Social Networks and Planned Organizational Change: The Impact of Strong Network Ties on Effective Change Implementation and Use. *J Appl Behav Sci*. 2003;39(3):281-300. doi:10.1177/0021886303258338

[4] Prell C. *Social Network Analysis: History, Theory and Methodology*. Sage Publications; 2012.

About the Authors

Kenneth Qua, is Research and Teaching Associate at the Institute for Digital Ecosystems, Department of Information Systems and Operations Management, Vienna University of Economics and Business.

Barbara Sporn is Professor and Director at the Institute for Higher Education Management, Vienna University of Economics and Business.

Singapore Management University (SMU): Tracking the Strategy Evolution of a Start-up University

MICHELLE LEE, HOWARD THOMAS AND ALEX WILSON

The year 2020 marked the 20th anniversary of the Singapore Management University (SMU). It would have been a year of festivities and indeed, the university's calendar was dotted with planned celebratory events. Many of those events, unfortunately, would not come to be as Covid-19 disrupted the rhythms of normal life. There would be no fanfare marking that milestone, but in its place, a quiet appreciation of how far the university has come and the labour of those who built it.

It was two years prior to SMU's 20th anniversary that we embarked on a project to document and track the strategic development of SMU since its founding. The aim was not to merely provide a historical reflection of events (for which at least one other book exists), but to provide an analysis of its strategic evolution, assessing the actors, decisions, and context at play in the strategic development of the university. The outcome of that effort is the book, "Creating a New Management University: Tracking the Strategy of Singapore Management University (SMU) in Singapore (1997–2019/20)" (Thomas, Wilson and Lee, 2022).

What prompted the writing of the book was not solely the occasion of the university's 20th anniversary; rather, it was the unique character of SMU, how it achieved take-off with a short runway, and its constant efforts at innovation over a two decade period that served as the impetus for offering a deep analysis of its strategies.

SMU exists in an ecosystem for higher education that is quite unlike what one might find in other parts of the world. The Singapore government provides ample funding to undergraduate programmes of local universities, but is unambiguous in conveying that its education mission is intertwined with its economic mission – that is, the universities are obliged to produce graduates that serve the needs of its economy. The supportive and stable environment the Singapore government provided in terms of its funding and policies meant a more predictable environment within which a university can make long-range planning. At the same time, the Singapore government was willing to loosen the reins on various aspects of SMU's governance and thus offered a degree of self-determination; for example, in matters of faculty recruitment and compensation, the university had autonomy. This provided a safe harbour, in a sense, for SMU to experiment with new ways of delivering a university education. Thus, SMU offers an interesting case study from which one might glean important insights.

While there may be many books that critically examine management education (e.g. Khurana, 2007; Thomas, Wilson, & Thomas, 2013; Lorange, 2019), few provide an in-depth look into a university's creation and strategic evolution. This book analyses secondary data and data from interviews with key individuals and synthesises many sources of evidence to draw conclusions about organisational leadership, strategies, patterns of strategic change, and performance outcomes as the university evolved through time. From our analysis, we identified four distinct strategic eras – distinctive time periods in SMU's strategic evolution – which are shown in Figure 1.

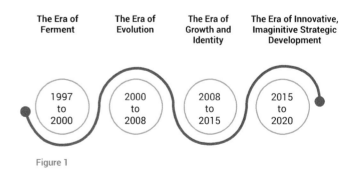

The Era of Ferment	The Era of Evolution	The Era of Growth and Identity	The Era of Innovative, Imaginitive Strategic Development
1997 to 2000	2000 to 2008	2008 to 2015	2015 to 2020

Figure 1

DOI: 10.4324/9781003390633-13

Global Focus **Annual Research** Volume 1

Singapore Management University (SMU): Tracking the Strategy Evolution of a Start-up University
Michelle Lee, Howard Thomas and Alex Wilson
....

ERA OF FERMENT (1997-2000)

The genesis of SMU begins in the phase that we have called the 'Era of Ferment', so named for the initial nebulous nature of the idea of establishing a new university, and the shifts and turns that preceded the eventual formation of SMU.

Singapore's development since its independence in 1965 has been undergirded by the belief that a strong educational system is the backbone of the country's economic development. It is therefore not surprising that the creation of a new university was an idea promulgated by the Singapore government and a key strategist involved in the formation of SMU was then Deputy Prime Minister (1995-2005), Dr. Tony Tan.

Pre-dating SMU were two full-fledged, public universities, the National University of Singapore (NUS) and Nanyang Technological University (NTU). By the second half of the 1990s, rising aspirations for higher education among the populace meant greater pressure to expand the number of university spaces. Meeting the greater demand could have been achieved by expanding the capacity of the two incumbent universities, but Dr. Tony Tan saw the opportunity to do something different. The prevailing perception of NUS and NTU graduates then – that they were good at rote learning but did not necessarily possess attributes such as strong communication skills, creative thinking, and global mindsets – may also have contributed to the decision to have a third university rather than simply expand the existing two.

It was decided that the new university would have a focus on management education; a decision that made sense in light of Singapore's growing strength as a financial centre and business hub. The plan was to convert an existing private institution that provided degree programmes in management, the Singapore Institute of Management (SIM), into a publicly-funded university. To further develop that plan, a governing council was constituted in 1997 and a prominent leader in the business community, Mr. Ho Kwon Ping, would serve as the chairperson of the council. Mr. Ho would take on that role with much fervour and is widely seen as another key strategist, alongside Dr. Tony Tan, in the development of SMU.

The new university was conceived as one that would be radically different from the two incumbent universities. For one thing, it would have a distinctive curriculum aimed at developing broader skill sets needed for Singapore to compete effectively in a rapidly globalising world. It later became apparent to the governing council, however, that the existing programmes of SIM would have to be radically changed if they were to achieve recognition as world-class programmes. The "major surgery" that would entail prompted serious consideration of the option of starting a new university from scratch. The moment that the council took the decision to abandon the idea of using SIM as a vehicle and to instead, create a brand new university, can perhaps be credited as the birth of SMU.

The design of SMU drew heavily upon the recommendations of the International Academic Advisory Panel (IAAP), a panel of prominent academics constituted by the Singapore government to provide advice on developing Singapore's higher education sector to become world class in terms of education and research. The panel recommended a different governance structure, one that would give universities greater autonomy in the management of funds provided by the government and greater flexibility in offering attractive remuneration packages that would help universities compete globally for academic talent. These recommendations served as the blueprint for SMU.

Freed from the constraints of working within existing structures, the governing council examined options for what the university might look like and what universities might serve as role models. Given the leading position of American universities in the world, there was a strong inclination towards emulating the American model and to depart from the British model upon which the incumbent universities were built. Also, given the management education focus, the council naturally looked to leading business schools for guidance. These strategic decisions led to the sealing of a partnership agreement in 1998 with the Wharton School of Business, an agreement that would impart a strong Wharton flavour to SMU's curriculum, pedagogy, research, recruitment strategy, and administration.

Global Focus **Annual Research** Volume 1

Singapore Management University (SMU): Tracking the Strategy Evolution of a Start-up University
Michelle Lee, Howard Thomas and Alex Wilson
....

On the matter of curriculum, Wharton's broad-based, liberal-focused model of education provided a distinctive model upon which to base SMU's first degree programme, the Bachelor of Business Management, and afforded a strong point of differentiation from programmes offered by the other two universities. The SMU curriculum, however, was not simply a carbon copy of the Wharton curriculum, but was adapted to account for the needs of the local student population. It was deemed important for students to acquire a global perspective, have strong communication skills, and understand the importance of service to the community, and the curriculum and pedagogy were thus designed with these goals in mind. An interactive pedagogy employed in a small class setting and the assignment of project work that culminated in presentations were employed to hone communication skills. Efforts were invested in sourcing for opportunities for overseas immersion in the form of exchange programmes and study missions. Community service and industry internships were made requirements for graduation. It was seen as imperative to build the capabilities of SMU students to become actively engaged with societal and business challenges and have pro-active, 'can-do' mindsets. All of these features of the curriculum allowed SMU to fill a clear gap in the market at the time and they continue to this day to be hallmarks of an SMU undergraduate education.

In 1999, Professor Janice Bellace from the Wharton School was appointed the first President of SMU. Appointing someone who was not from the local academic circles was seen as having the advantage of a clean slate upon which to build a new, entrepreneurial university. Professor Bellace had been involved in the formalisation of the SMU-Wharton partnership and her appointment as President further strengthened that nexus between the two institutions.

ERA OF EVOLUTION (2000-2008)

The Era of Evolution is a story of both implementation of the vision of the founding team and strategic emergence as the university fine-tuned its strategy. SMU would evolve from having a single school, the School of Business, to a multi-school, social science-based management university.

Following the appointment of Professor Bellace as President and the formal incorporation of SMU in 2000, the university's plans were implemented at a frenetic pace. Student recruitment was a matter of priority and intense efforts were directed at communicating SMU's value proposition to the marketplace. In keeping with the desire to develop students holistically, the admissions criteria were also holistic – a broad set of measures that would include academic qualifications (e.g. GCE A levels and SATs), interviews, essays, and assessments of leadership potential, as evidenced by involvement in co-curricular activities and prior work experience, were adopted.

For any student, the prospect of joining a start-up university with no record of past successes would be a risky undertaking, but the fact that the Singapore government and the Wharton School were 'backers' certainly gave assurance of credibility and quality. The value proposition of a broad-based education was also favourably received by the market. All of this was evidenced by the unexpectedly high number of applications received, with the number of applications far outstripping the number of places available. When the pioneering cohort of 300 students joined SMU in August 2000, the campus had the vibes of a start-up entity and these students would become co-creators of a vibrant student community.

Another immediate priority was to augment the pioneering team of faculty (who were involved in the early plans for SMU) with good quality faculty from the region and beyond. There would be movement of faculty from NUS and NTU to SMU, as some saw the opportunity to participate in a different model of governance, research, and education as an exciting one. These early faculty were mostly senior faculty with administrative experience, who were keen to get involved in shaping the new university. It was clear, however, that aggressive hiring efforts were needed overseas to build the faculty strength that was needed, particularly in research. Hence, SMU's presence at American conferences, where PhD candidates presented their research and interviewed for faculty positions was critical, as was the tapping of networks of contacts in the U.S. to spread the message about SMU. However, the pedagogical style of small class interactions meant the number of faculty needed could not be easily achieved with just this approach. Another phase of recruitment followed to fill this gap, this time focusing on faculty whose primary responsibility and expertise would be teaching - they would help enhance SMU's capabilities.

Global Focus **Annual Research** Volume 1

Singapore Management University (SMU): Tracking the Strategy Evolution of a Start-up University
Michelle Lee, Howard Thomas and Alex Wilson
....

In the first year of SMU's founding, there was just a single school, the School of Business, with two departments, business and accountancy. The university's aspiration, however, was to be a high-quality management school anchored in the social sciences and humanities, much like the London School of Economics in the U.K. It was thus necessary to develop faculty expertise and degree programmes in the allied disciplines of economics, social sciences, information systems, and law. The schools that would be launched in service of this goal occurred in rapid succession over the span of eight years.

The accountancy department was spun off as the School of Accountancy in 2001, largely because it was necessary, in the Singapore context, for accountancy programmes to be accredited by a professional body. This meant there had to be significant depth in accounting content in the curriculum, which made having accountancy exist simply as a major within the business degree programme untenable. This led to the launching of a second degree, the Bachelor of Accountancy, which also provided the opportunity for the university to offer the first double degree programme in business and accountancy in Singapore.

Economics and social sciences were seen as essential building blocks for a university that aspired to deliver a broad-based education and become a world-class institute of management. The School of Economics and Social Sciences was thus the next school to be launched in 2002. At about the same time, the university's leadership saw a market opportunity to 'marry IT with business' – there was demand for graduates with both a grounding in IT and an understanding of its applications to business. In response to this, the School of Information Systems was launched in 2003. The School of Law was the last school to be founded in 2007, even though it was identified early on as one of the schools that would be part of SMU's portfolio. Owing to the regulations that surround legal training in Singapore, there was a protracted period of planning for the school. As with the School of Information Systems that preceded it, the idea was for the law school to have a business bent. Finally, in 2007, the social science cluster within the School of Economics and Social Sciences was spun off to form a separate School of Social Sciences.

The overarching positioning of SMU as a research-focused university that also delivered innovative degree programmes would set the template for these schools, but each school's growth would be shaped by its Dean, faculty, and external partners. Schools were set up as independent business units and run as individual cost-centres, while the university played the role of a corporate parent, refining and negotiating school strategies while managing a portfolio of central services (administrative support, library, facilities management, etc.) for the schools.

By 2008, the full machinery of the six schools as envisioned by the founding leaders was in place, but what was so critical to oiling the machinery in these early years was the financial backing from the government. SMU was given generous funding in the form of an initial endowment, capital appropriations, and other operational funds that were comparable to those of leading research universities. The Singapore government also matched donations made by individuals and organisations to SMU three-to-one in the early years and one-to-one starting from 2005. An example of this would be the $150 million that the government committed to SMU, to match the donation of $50 million given by the Lee Foundation in 2004.

Importantly, SMU was given autonomy in how it allocated its funding to its initiatives and schools, the absence of which would have handicapped its ability to be innovative and responsive to shifting market conditions. The advantages of this independence cannot be overstated – it paved the way for the university to build an international reputation, by empowering its leadership to develop strategies for competing effectively.

Another factor that enabled SMU's growth, in terms of attracting faculty and students, was its campus in the city centre. It moved from its temporary campus, the Bukit Timah campus, to its much anticipated, permanent home in the Bras Basah precinct in 2005. This new campus is located on prime commercial land, land that Dr. Tony Tan had persuaded the cabinet to approve for SMU's campus. Both NUS and NTU are located in the outskirts of Singapore, so SMU's location close to the heart of business activity became an important point of differentiation.

ERA OF GROWTH AND IDENTITY (2008-2015)

By 2008, all signs were pointing to a university that was thriving – application numbers to SMU's programmes were strong, graduates were sought after by employers for being confident and articulate, and the university had attracted significant donation, including ones from the Lee Foundation and business tycoon and philanthropist, Li Ka Shing. In fact, the IAAP had described SMU as a "successful start-up", and then Minister of Education, Mr. Tharman Shanmugaratnam, described SMU as a start-up that competed with established players and got them to rethink what they were doing.

Following this early and rapid success was a phase where there was stronger focus on elevating the global standing of the university, generating high-quality research, and expanding its postgraduate offerings. This is the Era of Growth and Identity, an era led largely by Professor Arnoud De Meyer, who was SMU's fourth president from 2010 to 2019.

Global Focus **Annual Research** Volume 1

Singapore Management University (SMU): Tracking the Strategy Evolution of a Start-up University
Michelle Lee, Howard Thomas and Alex Wilson
....

Professor De Meyer had been the Director of the Judge Business School at Cambridge University from 2006 to 2010 and prior to that, the Founding Dean of INSEAD's Asia campus in Singapore from 1999 to 2002. His earlier experience in Singapore meant that he was well acquainted with the higher education landscape of Singapore and had clear ideas for the direction that SMU ought to take.

He consistently communicated the idea that SMU should aspire to be a management university that businesses and non-profit organisations would turn to for the best answer to their challenges, even if the answer might not be found within the confines of a traditional management discipline. That is, its endeavours ought to be centred around providing solutions to business and social problems, by drawing on knowledge and expertise that span multiple disciplines. This would, in fact, be almost revolutionary in the academic world, where there are well-entrenched incentives for faculty to build deep expertise in narrow fields. This cross-disciplinary approach, in his view, was needed not just in research, but in the way students were educated.

SMU's research centres and institutes would be the vehicles that would drive cross-disciplinary research. The number of such centres and institutes grew from six at the start of this era to 19 by the end of it and they were largely supported by funds from by companies and government agencies keen to support research with practical applications. SMU had also moved from a laissez faire approach to research to providing guidance to faculty on areas of research where there is potential for interdisciplinary teams to collaborate on impactful projects. Such programmes of research would have better odds of winning grants from publicly funded bodies, and success at winning such grants would, in turn, serve to enhance the research reputation of the university. Indeed, SMU received its first large-scale research grant awarded by the Ministry of Education for research on the economics of ageing in 2014, with funding amounting to $25 million.

Professor De Meyer also made expansion of programmes beyond SMU's undergraduate offering a strategic priority. SMU had built a strong brand in the undergraduate space, making it possible to leverage its brand in launching postgraduate, lifelong learning, and executive education programmes. This would make it a full-fledged management university capable of providing professional career development; thus, effectively positioning it as a university for the world of business. The number of postgraduate degree programmes grew from 11 to 34 across the six schools between 2008 and 2015, and the number of postgraduate students concomitantly tripled.

SMU was, however, cautious about losing its innovative edge, particularly with its undergraduate programme, and continued to examine and invest in new pedagogical approaches. One such innovation was a new category of experiential learning courses called SMU-X. Students worked on live projects with real clients under the mentorship of a faculty member. The aim was to have these projects make a real impact on the community using an interdisciplinary approach and a tripartite model of partnership between students, faculty, and industry professionals.

A final area of strategic priority was to build the global mindshare of SMU and burnish its reputation as a leading university in Asia, effectively moving it from the position of apprentice to leader. It would develop deep expertise in Asia, by conducting research relevant to the region and writing case studies about Asian businesses. The Centre for Management Practice, for example, was set up in 2011 to further this aim and in the first four years of its operation, produced about 150 case studies largely about Asian businesses. By building credibility as an expert on Asia, SMU would be sought out by universities, companies, and governments looking to make inroads in Asia.

SMU made significant headway in raising its international profile and by 2015, it had achieved a number of accolades – the School of Business became one of the youngest business schools to achieve accreditation by both AACSB and EFMD. It was ranked 4th in Asia and 49th worldwide in the UTD Top 100 Business School Research Ranking. The School of Economics was ranked 3rd in Asia and 67th worldwide in Tilburg University's Economics Research Ranking, and the School of Accountancy was ranked 1st in Asia and 22nd worldwide in the BYU Accounting Research Ranking.

Global Focus **Annual Research** Volume 1

Singapore Management University (SMU): Tracking the Strategy Evolution of a Start-up University
Michelle Lee, Howard Thomas and Alex Wilson

Towards the end of this era, there was a sense that SMU, despite its acknowledged success, was at an inflection point and that it needed to formalise a vision that would guide its development for the next ten years. Deliberations about its future culminated in Vision 2025, which outlined several aims.

The first is to enact SMU's role as "a game changer, through providing transformative education for a new generation of graduates" and that meant that SMU had to develop future-ready graduates, who possessed breadth and depth of knowledge, had a strong sense of ethics and social responsibility, were capable of solving real-world problems, and were, furthermore, articulate and self-initiating.

The second aim was for SMU to act as a catalyst in research and as "a source of cutting-edge research that integrates research with learning and practice". This meant that research should be supported by university seed money and multiplied through research grants, partnerships, and projects funded by both government and corporate partners.

The third aim was to be a global exemplar of an Asian city university by leveraging the university's city location to integrate itself with the business and local community. This would be achieved by undertaking projects that positively impact neighbouring communities and collaborating with businesses in tackling challenges. The university also had to widen its international footprint by building strong alliances with like-minded institutions around the world and though participation in global research and teaching networks.

ERA OF INNOVATIVE, IMAGINATIVE STRATEGIC DEVELOPMENT (2015-2020)

This era that we call the 'Era of Innovative, Imaginative Strategic Development' is one where strategic development was strongly guided by shared aims encapsulated in Vision 2025. This is also when a transition in leadership occurred, with the presidential reins passed from Professor De Meyer to Professor Lily Kong.

Professor Lily Kong is a cultural geographer by training and prior to joining SMU as Provost in 2015, was the Vice Provost (Academic Personnel) and Vice President (University and Global Relations) at Yale-NUS College. Her appointment signalled the importance that SMU placed on integrating the liberal arts into management education.

Indeed, an important strategic development that occurred in 2017 was a deep review of the undergraduate curriculum. A significant outcome of this review was a revamped Core Curriculum, structured as a set of 12 course units (out of a total of 36) that all SMU undergraduate students would have to take. A stronger emphasis on the humanities and social sciences is evident in the new Core Curriculum. Its three pillars of Capabilities, Communities, and Civilisations were designed to ensure that while students have the competencies to

dexterously operate in an increasingly complex, digitised, and data-driven working environment, they also have an understanding of the cultural, technological, and economic systems upon which communities are built, and have a keen awareness of issues that cut across space and time, such as ethics and social responsibility.

Other important changes that occurred in this time period include the launching of more interdisciplinary degrees and majors, such as the Bachelor of Science in Computing and Law programme, the Politics, Law, and Economics major, and the Health Economics and Management major. Both the broad-based, liberal arts model and the emphasis on interdisciplinary training helped to develop students with broader skill sets and the ability to traverse industries and jobs with ease.

It was also in this period that SMU made significant headway in the lifelong education space. In 2017, a new entity called SMU Academy was launched to integrate the activities of various campus units that were providing professional training programmes and create a seamless professional education service for corporate clients and government agencies. SMU Academy would also complement SMU's existing executive development – while the former would meet the needs of the continuing education segment, the latter would serve the customised executive education segment.

It is worth noting that the period from 2012 to 2018 saw little growth in executive education globally. At the same time, there was increased competition and price erosion in the customised executive education marketplace (for corporations and government entities) in Singapore. While SMU Executive Development (ExD) struggled with revenue growth targets given the challenging environment, there were growing numbers of professionals seeking continuing education. That growing demand was spurred by the provision of monetary grants, called SkillsFuture Credit, by the Singapore government, in an effort to get Singaporeans to engage in lifelong learning. The establishment of SMU Academy, therefore represented a systematic and coordinated approach to tapping that market.

To become a global exemplar for a city university, SMU created a series of International Advisory Councils in the region to build visibility and reputational capital through providing thought leadership. By building a council of influential business leaders in these countries, among them SMU alumni, the university hoped to gradually build a network of SMU ambassadors. Other outreach activities included speaker series and dialogue sessions (e.g. SMU Visionary series and City Dialogues) that served as platforms for connecting with the local community and for SMU to be a thought leader.

Global Focus **Annual Research** Volume 1

Singapore Management University (SMU): Tracking the Strategy Evolution of a Start-up University
Michelle Lee, Howard Thomas and Alex Wilson
....

Vision 2025 was given an update in September 2020, with the re-casting of some elements of the original strategic plan and a sharper focus on the priorities of the university. Renamed "SMU 2025", the update was described as necessary for better guiding the university into the second phase of its journey towards 2025. Of note is the identification of "Digital Transformation", "Sustainable Living", and "Growth in Asia" as priorities that the university would focus its efforts on. The strategies to achieve the university's vision remained as before; that is, "Transformative Education", "Cutting Edge Research", and "Engaged City University", as in Figure 2. Finally, the 4I's of "Integration", "Industry", "Innovation", and "Internationalisation" were identified as enablers that would differentiate the university and would be critical to its success (see Figure 2).

THE POST-COVID-19 FUTURE

The Covid-19 pandemic may have caused a slowdown in many spheres of life, but the pace of strategic developments at SMU continued unabated. Such was the intensity of commitment to Vision 2025. To be sure, there were initiatives that were accelerated by the pandemic because the pandemic made painfully clear the need for them. For example, investments were made in the area of blended learning – a clear framework, faculty training, and technical support were put in place to nudge faculty into offering courses in a blended learning format. Border restrictions and the suspension of travel meant that global exposure, a critical element of curricular and co-curricular programmes, was effectively nullified. Alternative ways of delivering global exposure, largely on virtual platforms, were assessed for rigour and then offered to students.

Other initiatives progressed at a blistering pace not because of the pandemic, but in spite of it. For example, SMU announced in June 2022 the launch of a new College of Integrative Studies. This new college would stand apart from the other six schools in offering students the flexibility of designing their own major under the mentorship of a faculty advisor and would confer a Bachelor of Integrative Studies. The aim is to develop integrative intelligence in students; that is, the ability to go beyond disciplinary boundaries to synthesise information surrounding an issue and draw upon knowledge in different domains to solve a problem. It would cater to students with particular interests for which existing 'canned' majors do not cater to. In addition, it would allow students to delay selection of a major until they had completed their first year of studies at SMU. This departs from the traditional model of admitting students into specific degree programmes; oftentimes, students enrol in a programme without necessarily having a good understanding of what it is about. The delayed selection of a major allows students to find their footing in university and get greater clarity about where their interests lie before committing to a particular programme of study.

Since its founding more than 20 years ago, SMU has not taken its foot off the pedal when it comes to rolling out initiatives in service of its strategic goals. For much of its history, it was a small, nimble entity in an environment conducive for growth. Maintaining that vigour in the years to come and resisting the lull of complacency will be a challenge that it will have to rise up to. But much hope remains that the entrepreneurial spirit will persist, if only because it has become very much the distinctive culture and character of SMU.

References

Khurana, R. (2007). *From higher aims to hired hands: The social transformation of American business schools and the unfulfilled promise of management as a profession*. Princeton, N.J.: Princeton University Press. (See pp.104-121, Business schools under fire: Humanistic management education as the way forward)

Lorange, P. (2019). *The business school of the future*. Cambridge, U.K.: Cambridge University Press

Thomas, H., Wilson, A., & Lee, M. (2022). *Creating a new management university: Tracking the strategy of Singapore Management University (SMU) in Singapore (1997-2019/20)*. Abingdon, U.K.: Routledge

About the Authors

Michelle P. Lee is an Associate Professor of Marketing (Education) and Associate Provost (Undergraduate Education) at Singapore Management University.

Howard Thomas is the Dean of Fellows at the British Academy of Management, Emeritus Professor at Singapore Management University and Senior Advisor at EFMD Global.

Alex Wilson is a Senior Lecturer in Strategy at Loughborough University, UK and a visiting academic at Singapore Management University.

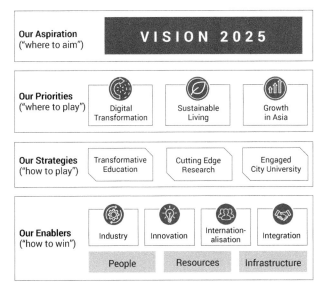

Figure 2

Striving for Meaningful Impact in and through Management Education: The IMD Perspective

JEAN-FRANÇOIS MANZONI

Over a twenty-five-year period I managed to skilfully avoid all significant academic leadership positions that came my way. I did so because I had noticed early on that Deans are severely limited in their ability to engage in the activities that led most of us to choose an academic career, and they lose a considerable proportion of their freedom and control over their time, an aspect of academic life that was most precious to me.

And yet, in 2016, I agreed to "throw my hat in the ring" and later accepted the Board's offer to succeed my colleague Dominique Turpin at the helm of the *International Institute for Management Development*, better known under its acronym IMD. I agreed to do so because I profoundly believe in IMD's distinctive purpose and modus operandi, and I believe in the impact we have on the world. Let me try to explain why.

IMD IN A NUTSHELL

First, it is important to describe briefly our legal nature and the fundamentals of our economic model: IMD is an independent academic institution - a not-for-profit, stand-alone business school operated as a private Foundation governed by a Foundation Board (50 members) that delegates its day-to-day authority to an 8–10-member Supervisory Board. The IMD Foundation originated about thirty years ago from the merger between two similar "independent academic institutions", IMEDE and IMI. Importantly, both IMEDE and IMI had initially been created by major multinationals as executive education providers (Alcan in 1946 for IMI and Nestlé in 1957 for IMEDE). Coincidentally, both institutions started offering MBA degrees in 1972, a bit less than 20 years before they were merged by their respective Boards.

IMD is triple-accredited and tends to enjoy relatively flattering rankings for its programmes. Our MBA programme, for example, was selected as the #1 programme in Europe in BloombergBusinessWeek's last four rankings and as the #1 international one-year MBA programme in four of the last five Forbes rankings. Our EMBA programme was ranked in the world's top 10 in the last three rankings of The Economist. And the Financial Times has positioned us in the top three world-wide for its last 10 Executive Education global rankings, and in the top five for the last 18 rankings (a feat accomplished by only two schools in the world).

One last point about us: Our degree programmes generate about 20% of our revenues, with the remaining 80% being almost entirely generated by non-degree activities mainly composed of open and custom executive education programmes. About 2% of our revenues are generated by "fundraising" activities (mainly Chairs that are being drawn-down over an agreed-upon number of years).

In this context, we use two key statements to describe who we are and why we exist.

Who we are: "Founded by business executives for business executives, we are an independent academic institution with Swiss roots and global reach. We strive to be the trusted learning partner of choice for ambitious individuals and organisations worldwide."

Our purpose/mission: "Challenging what is and inspiring what could be, we develop leaders who transform organisations and contribute to society."

DOI: 10.4324/9781003390633-14

These two statements have several important implications for us:

- We do think of ourselves as educators first and foremost. *Our most direct impact on the world is the impact we have on the students and executives who attend our programmes.*

- As a result, we take pedagogy very seriously. We discuss it a lot and we have written a number of books to document and share our expertise, including Strebel and Keys (2005) and Anand & Barsoux (2014).

- With hardly any exception, IMD's faculty members were "star instructors" in the institutions they left to join us, and their experience joining us is typically that they now have to "up their game" to rise to the excellence level of most of their colleagues. "Upping their game" involves investing more time and energy preparing and delivering their sessions, including through learning from colleagues.

- Colleagues do help one another for several reasons: a) Collaborativeness is one of three non-negotiable qualities at hiring. (The other two are smart and passionate about what we do &/or what they do.) b) We tend to have more work than we can handle, which means that each of us can typically yield more benefits from having a few additional capable colleagues around to help in programmes than from withholding support in order hopefully to "remain on top". c) Most of us direct programmes, which means that we need colleagues to "teach in our programmes". This creates a high degree of interdependence, which means that the group has easy ways of penalizing individuals who would not behave collaboratively.

- Importantly, IMD faculty members understand the economic incentives associated with excellence in programme direction and teaching. Individually, they can increase their own compensation by accepting to "sell back to the school" some of the 50 personal days afforded in their contract. The programme staffing process is not completely decentralised, but it does have some market-like properties and most successful instructors tend to have more opportunities to increase their income. Collectively, IMD faculty members are eligible to a "variable compensation system" that gets funded by the financial surplus we create together (in most years). About 40% of this pool is distributed based on research performance, with the other 60% of this pool distributed based on variables positively correlated with teaching &/or programme direction quality and quantity.

- Unsurprisingly in the context of the above, it is fair to say that IMD faculty members tend to spend a greater proportion of their time in class and preparing for class than most tenure-track faculty members at top schools.

A RESOLUTE FOCUS ON IMPACT IN EVERYTHING WE DO

When I re-joined IMD in 2016, we were still using a tag line that had served us well for years: *Real World, Real Learning*. I proposed to my colleagues to change it to *Real Learning, Real Impact*. Two major reasons were underlying this proposal:

First, the term "real world" was increasingly sounding "old economy", especially for younger generations who often interpreted it as referring to industrial activities. Secondly, we could clearly sense that executives and corporate clients were becoming increasingly demanding in terms of executive development programmes having a *substantial* and *sustained* impact on participants. They acknowledged that managers returning from executive programmes came back energised and full of good intentions, but lamented that these good intentions tended to be short lived and too many managers tended to revert back too quickly to usual practice.

The faculty meeting discussion was generally supportive, but I do remember a colleague intervening to say: "But Jean-François, if we change the tag line to promise impact, we're then going to have to deliver on this promise!". This astute observation was followed by a long silence, which I broke to reply: "That's exactly why we must commit to it. It will force us to up our game in order to deliver".

In line with the impact framework developed by efmd and proposed under the BSIS label (see Kalika (2022) and Manzoni et al. (2020)), we tend to discuss our impact in terms of five different domains:

1. Executives and organisations through our programmes
2. Executives and organisations through our research
3. Management education, through the pedagogical material we create and make available to other schools
4. Public policy, through our research and programmes with some governments
5. Regional and Swiss ecosystem, through our financial impact and work with start-ups and scale-ups.

Let me take each of these domains in turn.

1. Impact on managers and organisations through our programmes

As mentioned above, we believe that our programmes are the most direct way for us to have an impact on the world. We cannot assert that it is our "largest impact", because we have no way of calibrating the various areas of impact we have. But our programmes are undoubtedly our most direct impact on the world through their impact on degree programme students (who go on to become managers), managers and organisations.

Regrettably, we don't yet have a perfect way to assess the impact of these programmes, so we use a range of direct and indirect assessments.

Direct assessments include a range of data collected at the end of the modules/programmes and again four months later. These data tend to be student-provided, with the advantages and disadvantages of such data. We are working hard at developing non-self-reported impact measures, but these approaches tend to require more time and investment from executives and corporate clients, and so far we are not yet getting enough support from them to push the process as far as we would like to push it. We just hired a new "Head of Impact Assessment" to accelerate our progress.

Indirect assessments include alumni's delayed attitude toward the school and corporate clients' willingness to work with us again. This willingness to work again, likely informed by their perception of how successfully previous interventions met their objectives, is very important for us given our dependency on executive programme revenues. Executive programme participants' and corporate partners' perceptions are also very much driving the annual Financial Times Executive Education global rankings, in which we tend to do well as mentioned above.

We also apply for "executive education awards", including the EFMD/EQUIS *Excellence in Practice* Awards. These awards are attributed by sophisticated juries based on detailed cases submitted by the various schools and corporate clients. This year we won one Gold and one Silver awards (i.e., 25% of the awards attributed across the 4 categories), as well as several similar awards from other organisations.

2. Impact on managers and organisations through our research

Almost thirty years ago, while serving on the faculty of another school, I attended a talk by a professor who held a joint appointment at that school and at a top US School. His presentation started with "the purpose of business schools is to produce research". I immediately raised my hand and asked, "is that what it is?" He paused and replied thoughtfully: "Good question. I guess it has been at every school I have been a part of."

Nobody at IMD would say that our purpose is to produce research. As mentioned above, our purpose is *to develop leaders who transform organisations and contribute to society*, and one of our key levers to do so is to *challenge what is and inspire what could be*. For the overwhelming majority of IMD faculty, then, research is not an end in itself; it is a means to an end, where the end is "to develop leaders who ..." .

Research is, clearly, an important means to that end. First, conducting research keeps us intellectually alive and alert, focused on questions and curious about the world and how it functions. We can't challenge what is and inspire what could be in others if we don't do so for ourselves. Secondly, research is a natural outgrowth of IMD faculty's typically intense curiosity and our continuous contacts with executives and organisations, who come to us with problems and questions for which we often don't have a clear answer and which we are hence prompted to study. Much of the research conducted at IMD starts from questions raised in class.[1] Last but not least, producing quality research is also a way for us to convince executives and organisations that they should choose to attend programmes with us rather than another provider.

One of our challenges on the research front is the fact that our faculty tends to be pretty busy with acquiring, designing &/or delivering executive programmes. Another disadvantage is the absence of a PhD programme, which is often a significant lever for faculty's research productivity. We try to compensate for these challenges by allocating very significant financial resources to supporting our faculty's efforts – between 8% and 10% of our revenues is allocated to out-of-pocket research support costs (i.e., not counting faculty time).

Unsurprisingly given our focus on education, we tend to think of research in broader terms than most top schools. For us, research should aim to be *rigorous, relevant, insightful* and *actionable*. We understand that these four dimensions sometimes require trade-offs, but we typically attribute more value than other schools to the latter three criteria. As a result, we probably value more than other schools the production of books, cases and articles published in practitioner outlets. On the latter front, for example, IMD tends to rank very highly in terms of presence in *Harvard Business Review* and *Sloan Management Review* (the only two practitioner-focused outlets included in the so-called "FT 50" list)[2]. For example, we were the 4th most frequently appearing institution in 2016-2020 and we ranked 3rd for 2017-2021 – keeping in mind that the two schools most frequently appearing in these journals are the two schools that publish them.

We do encourage and keep track of more academic publications, as represented in Exhibit 1. In fact, we decided a few years ago that we needed to increase our collective investment in academic research, including and particularly when published in top academic outlets. This led us to broaden the diversity of our faculty, as represented in Exhibit 2. Historically, IMD tended to hire faculty members characterised by a balanced profile in terms of academic focus vs. connection to practice. Over the last few years we have welcomed a few colleagues whose profile is more heavily tilted toward one of the two poles.

These new hires are important for us and we work hard at integrating and encouraging them. But the vast majority of IMD faculty members remains practice-oriented academics with a strong commitment to our purpose and their role therein.

3. Impact on management education through the use of our pedagogical material by other institutions

From a pedagogical point of view, IMD is not per se a "case school" (that would rely 100% on case studies being discussed in a traditional "case discussion process"). We also use a wide range of pedagogical approaches including lecture/discussions, simulations and experiential activities. Nevertheless, we do use pedagogical cases and allocate a substantial amount of R&D funding to the production of case studies.

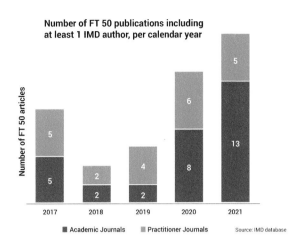

Number of FT 50 publications including at least 1 IMD author, per calendar year

■ Academic Journals ■ Practitioner Journals   Source: IMD database

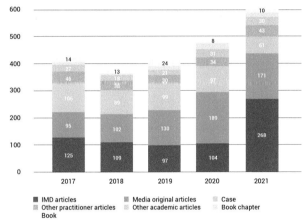

Number of other publications per calendar year

Copyright © 2022 IMD. All rights reserved

Exhibit 1 Tracking IMD research activities over time

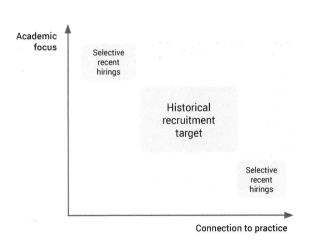

Exhibit 2 Recent evolution of the faculty portfolio

To assess our impact on this front, we track three types of indicators:

a) How many of our cases are bought by instructors in other institutions?

In 2021, for example, over 200,000 IMD cases were sold to more than 1,300 institutions in 111 countries.

b) How many of our colleagues are able to develop "best-selling" (and hence influential) cases?

For example, in 2020-2021 we had six colleagues among the Case Center's Top 50 best-selling authors and nine colleagues had at least one case appearing in the best-selling &/or classic cases lists.

c) How many of our cases are winning awards (i.e., are selected by a relevant jury as a high-quality pedagogical asset)?

The main case awards are of course that attributed by efmd and the Case Center, but we also track our performance in case competitions like the John Molson MBA International Case Writing Competition or the HEC Montréal Corporate Social Responsibility Case Writing Competition. We also track who wins these awards, including in terms of generations of faculty members. It is important for us that more recently hired colleagues start succeeding their older colleagues in these areas.

4. Public Policy

As mentioned above, IMD was founded by executives for executives. We are hence not naturally as focused on policy making as other schools such as the Geneva Graduate Institute or graduate schools of government / public policy in top universities. Nonetheless, we understand the importance of policy making for the world and particularly the world of business.

Our World Competitiveness Center (https://www.imd.org/centers/world-competitiveness-center) has established proprietary and respected methodologies to produce annual rankings of countries in terms of their overall competitiveness, their ability to attract, retain and develop talent, and their digital readiness. These rankings attract attention from many governments around the world and often get discussed by relevant groups of executives and policy makers.

We also get a number of requests to work with governments to support their policy making reflections and by civil service training organisations to help them develop the capabilities of their country's civil servants.

5. Impact on the regional and national economy

Last and proverbially not least, and thanks to the methodology we acquired through the BSIS accreditation, we have been tracking more systematically our short- and longer-term impacts on the regional and national economy.

Short term, the BSIS methodology enabled us to quantify IMD's direct and indirect impact on the regional economy. We were very surprised by how large this impact was, as were local and regional policy makers; they — and we - had heretofore considerably under-estimated our impact on the regional economy.

Medium- to longer-term, one of IMD's key contributions to the regional and national economy occurs through our work with start-ups and scale-ups. Every year, we run a start-up competition to select about 30 start-ups that will benefit from the support of a team of MBA or EMBA students as a significant component of their programme. The start-ups supported by the EMBA get to go to Silicon Valley for a week and often return to Switzerland with additional financing. We track what happens to the start-ups that we help and we know, for example, that two of them are now Unicorns and that we have worked with 40 of the "2021 best 100 Swiss start-ups".[3] In partnership with the governmental organisation supporting innovation, we have also launched a programme that enables us to support scale-ups over a one year process.

Global Focus **Annual Research** Volume 1

Striving for Meaningful Impact in and through Management Education: The IMD Perspective
Jean-François Manzoni
....

ENABLERS OF THIS RESOLUTE FOCUS ON IMPACT IN ALL OUR ACTIVITIES

It is clear to us – IMD faculty, staff, foundation and supervisory boards – that we are quite different from most business schools we know, particularly from business schools belonging to universities and hence operating under much more constraining rules and regulations than we do.

IMD's historical functioning – and the conditions that enabled it to function that way – have been analysed in substantial detail in Lorange (2002 and 2008) and Manzoni (2008). There have obviously been some changes over the last 15-20 years, but IMD's fundamental positioning and functioning are still quite similar to what they were then. To this day, the characteristics that help IMD to operate in a very purpose-centric way (with its very education-centric purpose) include:

- A very tight governance structure, including clear faculty and staff representation as one would expect in an academic institution, but wherein the IMD Dean (actually called President) wields more authority than most Deans, and does so under the supervision of a small and engaged Board of Directors.
- IMD is an independent academic institution, and hence not subject to the constraints that come from being part of a larger university. As a result, all decisions made at IMD – from faculty hiring and promotion to the allocation of various types of resources - are made by and for the benefit of the business school.
- IMD's faculty does not have departments or academic areas; there is one faculty group, all reporting if you will to IMD's Faculty Dean and President. This system is quite demanding for these individuals (e.g., in January and February the Faculty Dean and the President must meet each of IMD's 50+ colleagues for a one-hour meeting), but it significantly reduces politics and fragmented agendas.
- IMD faculty's "open contracts" offer them some long-term protection, but significantly less than the traditional tenure system. IMD faculty members know that they must work hard at remaining productive contributors for the institution. If they don't, their job is at risk but - probably more importantly to them -, so is their standing and relationship with their colleagues.
- IMD's faculty and staff have a strong shared understanding of the school's purpose, economic model, culture and values. We very actively nurture this shared sense of destiny and direction, and it represents a significant advantage in terms of IMD remaining a purpose-centric institution with a strong focus on Real Learning and Real Impact for managers and organisations.

CONCLUDING REMARKS

IMD's independence has significant advantages in terms of simplicity and focus. Combined with our lack of substantial endowment, this independence also presents us with a challenge every year to generate enough revenues to cover – without any help from anyone - all the costs associated with running an academic institution in today's world. For the vast majority of business schools, degree programmes contribute to creating a relatively stable (and somewhat counter cyclical) revenue profile. At IMD, degree programmes are smaller than most other institutions' and we must hence generate more than 75% of our revenues anew every year.

In effect and until we develop an endowment, we at IMD are sentenced to being - and to being perceived by managers and organisations as – relevant and positively impactful. In fact, as more relevant and impactful than other schools and professional service firms that these individuals and organisations can choose to address their needs.

I think that building on the great work of our predecessors, we have made a virtue out of necessity. We have created a set of mechanisms and an organisational culture that helps us to be very aligned in the pursuit of our shared purpose   challenging what is and inspiring what could be, we develop leaders who transform organisations and contribute to society. This focus very much determines our approach to everything we do, including faculty hiring and management as well as research and pedagogical material development.

Our model clearly won't suit everyone; it is certainly not for the faint of heart, especially when – as in January 2020 and the appearance of the Covid 19 pandemic – revenues from face-to-face executive education suddenly dropped like a rock! But once more, we stayed on purpose, we committed to – and succeeded at - innovating fast and furiously and we radically transformed our delivery model (see Manzoni, 2022a). Our faculty & staff agreed to substantial sacrifices, while our Board agreed to let us continue to invest in key areas (see Manzoni, 2022b). Thanks to all these elements we are coming out of the Covid crisis a stronger organisation, powered by strong momentum and a renewed determination to do our best every day to contribute as much as we can to the development of a more prosperous, sustainable and inclusive world.

Global Focus **Annual Research** Volume 1

Striving for Meaningful Impact in and through Management Education: The IMD Perspective
Jean-François Manzoni
....

Footnotes

[1] An important note: This ongoing contact with demanding executives and organisations also forces IMD faculty to stay very much up-to-date with research conducted elsewhere, for which in many cases they act as translators to an audience of practitioners (for which the research was not initially conducted and written up).

[2] https://www.ft.com/content/3405a512-5cbb-11e1-8f1f-00144feabdc0

[3] https://www.imd.org/news/updates/TOP-100-Swiss-Startups-2021/

References

Anand, N. and J-L Barsoux (2014) *QUEST: Leading Global Transformations*. Lausanne: IMD International

Kalika, M. (2022) https://blog.efmdglobal.org/2022/06/01/bsis-a-decade-of-impact/

Lorange, P. (2002) *New vision for management education: Leadership challenges*. Oxford: Pergamon Press.

Lorange, P. (2008) *Thought leadership meets business: How business schools can become more successful*. Cambridge: Cambridge University Press.

Manzoni, J-F. (2008) "On the Folly of Hoping for A, Simply Because You're (Trying to) Pay for A", in *Performance Measurement and Management Control: Measuring and Rewarding Performance*, Marc J. Epstein and Jean-François Manzoni, Editors (Emerald, 2008), pp. 19-41

Manzoni, J-F., A-F. Borgeaud-Pierrazzi and E. Neutuch (2020) "Real Learning, Real Impact: Exploring the impact of an International Business School with the EFMD Business School Impact System", *EFMD Global Focus* (Vol. 14, #2 (April 2020), pp. 4-8)

Manzoni, J-F. (2022a) "Executive Education Post-Pandemic: Reflections on the Role of Technology-Mediated Interactions Going Forward", in *Executive Education after the Pandemic: A Vision for the Future*, Santiago Iniguez and Peter Lorange, Editors (Palgrave, 2022), pp. 245-256

Manzoni, J-F. (2022b) "Leading an (Unusual) Academic institution through a Crisis: A Personal Reflection", in *Business School Leadership and Crisis: Exit Planning* (Global Deans' Contributions on the Occasion of the 50th Anniversary of the EFMD), Eric Cornuel, Editor (Cambridge University Press, 2022), pp. 311-330

Strebel, P. and S. Keys (2005) *Mastering Executive Education: How to Combine Content with Context and Emotion - The IMD Guide*. Paul Strebel and Tracy Keys, Editors (FT Prentice Hall, 2005)

About the Author

Jean-François Manzoni is the President of the International Institute for Management Development (IMD), where he also serves as the Nestlé Professor of Leadership and Organisational Development.